John Bunyan

THE PEOPLE'S PILGRIM

CWR

Published 2013 by CWR, Waverley Abbey House, Waverley Lane, Farnham, Surrey GU9 8EP, UK. CWR is a Registered Charity – Number 294387 and a Limited Company registered in England – Registration Number 1990308.

For a list of our National Distributors visit www.cwr.org.uk/distributors

Unless otherwise indicated, all Scripture references are from the Holy Bible: New International Version (NIV), copyright © 1973, 1978, 1984 by the International Bible Society.

Other version marked:
AV: The Authorised Version

Concept development, editing, design and production by CWR
Photos on pages 117 and 122 taken by James White and used by permission of Saltmine Trust
Printed in China by 1010

ISBN: 978-1-85345-836-1

Who could have predicted that a ragged, impoverished, foul-mouthed tinker-mechanic would live to pen the bestselling novel of all time – *The Pilgrim's Progress* – its blockbuster sales second only to the Bible itself? Bunyan's life as Morden narrates it is history at its most entertaining, full of insight, surprise, tension, courage and awesome endurance. Bunyan's fraught journey amid hostile seventeenth-century intolerance and injustice, resonates with our times too, as religious bigotry – secular and sectarian – seeks to silence or imprison outspoken believers today. John Bunyan is our role-model 'Mr Stand-fast' whose life-work grips and inspires us. Who says the Puritans were dull? This enthralling and illustrated biography proves otherwise.

Greg Haslam, Minister of Westminster Chapel, London

Peter Morden has produced another winning biography. In this vivid life story, we discover the secret of Bunyan's enduring power to touch the heart with spiritual encouragement that emanates from his experience of hardship and suffering. John Bunyan's personal progress as a pilgrim has immense contemporary relevance for those who feel marginalised by society because of their Christian convictions. Read *The People's Pilgrim* and *you* will be less likely to quit until your journey is over!

David Coffey OBE, Global Ambassador for BMS World Mission

This book provides a fascinating and detailed insight into the life and background of John Bunyan. Although living conditions were totally different in the seventeenth century, the author cleverly transposes the stories of Bunyan's challenges to parallel with our own today. The results are thought-provoking and inspiring!

Fiona Castle OBE, writer and speaker

Accessible, scholarly, challenging and inspirational! Peter Morden's easy style draws you into the harsh world of seventeenth-century England and brings vividly to life underlying challenges and opportunities in our own lives as seen through the life of John Bunyan. A time in the history of our land of immense struggle for religious freedom, without which we would not enjoy such openness and opportunity today. Bunyan Meeting Church today as a member of the Congregational Federation remains, along with a rich family of other Christian churches as a living expression of such needed dissent, reliance upon God and courage to continue to follow a way that has become seemingly so alien to today's society.

John Bunyan's unique story is one of many such folk from those years for whom the pursuit of faith demanded everything. Peter gives us dramatic insights into the motivations of Bunyan's writings, now famous imagined places and peoples drawn from great biblical themes and chapters of all our lives.

I tremendously enjoyed this book for it never trivialised or glamorised the life that Bunyan lived and thus will enable, I believe, anyone who reads it to find a genuine resonance, tremendous encouragement and ultimately, hope. Reflective sections at the end of each chapter are an essential part, asking, as they do, some quite searching questions to release in our own life something of the deep-rooted hope Bunyan himself lived and wrote for.

I suspect this book will, as it has for me, have you reading more of Bunyan and reading more into your own life and purposes.

Rev Michael Heaney, General Secretary Congregational Federation, Moderator of the Free Churches Group, Co-President of Churches Together in England

CONTENTS

Foreword   7

Personal Note   8

Introduction   9

1. Background and Early Experiences   17

2. Conviction and Conversion   33

3. Travelling Through the Storm: 49
   Grace Abounding to the Chief of Sinners

4. Ministry Begins   67

5. Arrest, Trial and Imprisonment   79

6. Surviving and Thriving: Life in Prison   93

7. *The Pilgrim's Progress*   107

8. Bunyan the Pastor   129

9. Two More Stories: 145
   The Holy War and *The Pilgrim's Progress: Part 2*

10. The Final Journey   167

Conclusion: The Influence of John Bunyan   183

Acknowledgements   189

Endnotes   191

FOREWORD

I was deeply moved as I read *John Bunyan: The People's Pilgrim*, and realised how little I actually knew about this amazing man and the difficult period of history in which he lived. I was booked to preach in Bedford around the same time I was reading this, so that was very special. I recommend that those who read this book try to visit Bedford, especially the museum dedicated to John Bunyan.

This book is important to me as we at OM (Operation Mobilisation) have distributed thousands of copies of *The Pilgrim's Progress* in many forms around the world. It is my hope that those who read this book will want to read (or have already read) that great classic.

Never did I believe that we would come to a day when so few people even know the name John Bunyan, especially outside the walls of the church. My prayer is that many who don't go to church may still find this book unique and interesting; certainly people interested in English history will find it special. I hope people will get a few extra copies to give away to their friends.

One of the powerful messages of this book is how God works within the culture of the day and how in the midst of so many difficulties, He continues His work of grace. Yes, here is a great man with all his humanness who manifested the GRACE of God. That's my prayer for those who take the time to read this special book about such a unique and special person.

Dr George Verwer
2012

TO ANNE, WITH ALL MY LOVE

PERSONAL NOTE

Half way through writing this book my wife Anne was diagnosed with breast cancer. I have watched her come through a difficult operation and subsequently undergo a gruelling course of chemotherapy treatment, followed by radiotherapy. It has been a hard journey indeed. John Bunyan's suffering was in some ways quite different to hers, but his example of keeping close to God in tough times has encouraged and sustained us both. There were a number of occasions when I considered weaving our own experiences into *The People's Pilgrim*, but after some hesitation and a few false starts I have decided against that. This is mainly because the book really ought to focus on John Bunyan and the ways God worked in him and through him, not on us. But also – if I'm completely honest – the events of Anne's illness are still too close and painful for me to write about in a clear and connected way. Nevertheless, our own questions and struggles do stand behind my writing in the 'application' sections of some of the chapters. We thank God for the amazing peace and strength He has given us and we face the future as a couple full of faith and hope knowing, as I said at one point in Chapter Seven, that 'our times are in His hands'.

This book is dedicated to the brave and beautiful Anne, with immense gratitude for twenty-one years of very special pilgrimage together and looking forward, God willing, to many more years ahead.

Peter J. Morden
Spurgeon's College
August 2012

INTRODUCTION

FROM PREACHER TO PRISON ...

On 12 November 1660, John Bunyan travelled the short distance from his home in Bedford to the tiny hamlet of Lower Samsel, where he was due to preach. The group that had come together for worship was small, numbering no more than forty people. Like many such rural congregations, they had no church building. In the summer they would often meet outdoors under a hawthorn tree in some woods, but this was a cold November day and so they had gathered in a farmhouse to await Bunyan's arrival. They were ordinary men and women, many of them poor and unschooled. Their speaker also had little by way of formal education. He was a simple tradesman, a tinker or brazier, someone who eked out a living making and mending pots, pans and kettles. But he was known in the locality as a lively, effective preacher, and as he arrived at Lower Samsel he knew what the subject of his message would be. He was going to speak, as simply and as clearly as he could, about the need for faith in Jesus Christ. All this might seem harmless enough. However, meetings like this had been declared illegal by the government. And on this day the preacher was in particular danger.

As Bunyan entered the house he noticed the small congregation

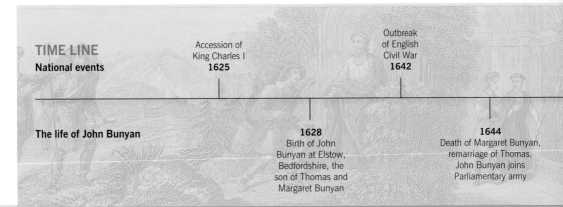

TIME LINE

National events

Accession of King Charles I
1625

Outbreak of English Civil War
1642

The life of John Bunyan

1628
Birth of John Bunyan at Elstow, Bedfordshire, the son of Thomas and Margaret Bunyan

1644
Death of Margaret Bunyan, remarriage of Thomas. John Bunyan joins Parliamentary army

was especially tense and nervous. He soon learned why. It was rumoured the authorities knew where they were meeting and, what's more, that a warrant had been issued for the preacher's arrest. What should they do? It was suggested they just abandon the service. Why take such a risk when they could simply disperse and then meet in secret on some other occasion? Bunyan went outside for a moment to consider his options. After a brief struggle with his feelings he determined they should go ahead with the meeting. He had often spoken about the need for courage in the face of persecution; now he had to back up his words with deeds. Bravely he turned and walked back towards the house.

The meeting began with prayer, but before they could go any further the local constable and another man burst in to arrest Bunyan. There was no time for the prepared message, but before he was led away he did manage to shout out a few words of encouragement to the frightened people. He told them to be of 'good cheer' for they had not done anything wrong. Rather they were being persecuted for their faith. They shouldn't be discouraged but instead press on to know Jesus better. Before he could say any more, he was hustled out of the building into the cold November air.

Right:
Statue of John
Bunyan, Bedford

... FROM PRISONER TO PILGRIM

Bunyan's dramatic experience seems out of the ordinary to us, but it was not unusual in seventeenth-century England. Similar

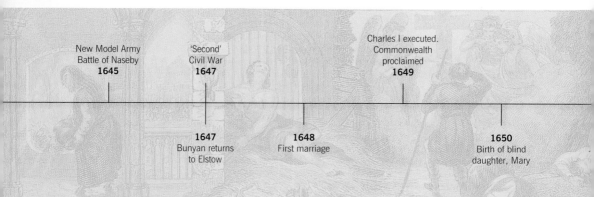

New Model Army
Battle of Naseby
1645

'Second'
Civil War
1647

Charles I executed.
Commonwealth
proclaimed
1649

1647
Bunyan returns
to Elstow

1648
First marriage

1650
Birth of blind
daughter, Mary

scenes were being played out across the length and breadth of the land as Christian meetings were broken up and church leaders brought for trial. And this is where the story of John Bunyan might have ended, for he could have been deported from the country for his so-called crimes, or even executed. As it was, he was imprisoned in Bedford Jail for nearly twelve years because he steadfastly refused to give an undertaking to stop preaching. Held in squalid, cramped conditions, he shared the prison with common criminals and lived with the knowledge he might never be released. Some Christian leaders simply died in jail. Given the overcrowded, unhealthy conditions of these prisons and the cruelty with which many inmates were treated, this was hardly surprising.

Yet John Bunyan survived and, more than that, he used his time in prison wisely. In particular, he wrote a wide range of books including the one for which he is best known, *The Pilgrim's Progress*. Somehow, confined in his dirty, damp prison cell with little outside stimulus, Bunyan managed to pen one of the acknowledged classics of English literature. In *The Pilgrim's Progress* Bunyan vividly describes the journey of 'Christian' as he travels through such perils as the 'Slough of Despond' and 'Vanity Fair' towards the 'Celestial City'.

First Anglo-Dutch War **1652**	Oliver Cromwell becomes Lord Protector **1653**	England divided into eleven military districts **1655**		Death of Oliver Cromwell **1658**
1652 Bunyan's conversion	**1653** Joins independent congregation meeting at St John's Church, Bedford	**1655** Bunyan family resident in St Cuthbert's Street, Bedford	**1656** Publication of Bunyan's first book, *Some Gospel Truths Opened*	**1658** Death of first wife

This lively parable or allegory of the Christian life was first published in 1678, with a second part following in 1684. It made its author something of a celebrity in his own lifetime, but it was after his death the popularity of *The Pilgrim's Progress* took off and the book became a worldwide phenomenon. Today it stands as the

world's second most printed book – only the Bible has been published more often. Bunyan wrote many other works too. A number of these were based on sermons he had given and this reminds us, when he was finally let out of prison, that he boldly continued his preaching. Towards the end of his life thousands flocked to hear him, particularly when he was visiting London and able to use larger venues. The Puritan theologian John Owen once said he would give up all his immense learning in exchange for the 'tinker's power to touch [people's] hearts'. This simple, working-class tradesman, locked up for preaching to a small handful of people, became one of the most influential Christians Britain has ever produced. The story of *The Pilgrim's Progress* and the way it was, and still is, read around the world is remarkable. The story of Bunyan's own personal 'pilgrimage' is no less astonishing.

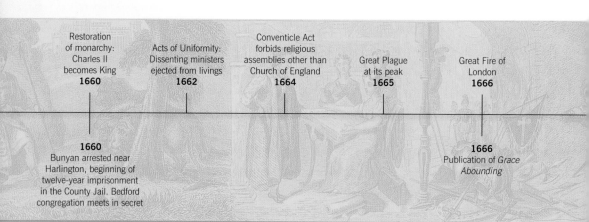

| Restoration of monarchy: Charles II becomes King **1660** | Acts of Uniformity: Dissenting ministers ejected from livings **1662** | Conventicle Act forbids religious assemblies other than Church of England **1664** | Great Plague at its peak **1665** | Great Fire of London **1666** |

1660
Bunyan arrested near Harlington, beginning of twelve-year imprisonment in the County Jail. Bedford congregation meets in secret

1666
Publication of *Grace Abounding*

ABOUT THIS BOOK

What I aim to do in this book is tell Bunyan's extraordinary story. Of course, this will include looking at some of his different publications, not just *The Pilgrim's Progress*, but other classics such as *The Holy War*, as well as lesser known works on important subjects like prayer and suffering. Bunyan had tremendous sympathy with the struggles that ordinary men and women faced. He was able to relate the Christian faith to such people in a lively way and with great sympathy and insight. His books have shaped the spirituality of countless Christians on every continent and they have the potential to speak powerfully to a new generation of believers too. Do you want to know more about prayer, dealing with discouragement, keeping going when the going gets tough, using your gifts, growing in holiness, or engaging in spiritual warfare? If so, the writings of John Bunyan are for you.

My primary aim, however, has been to write about Bunyan the man and chronicle his own extraordinary life journey. Who was the person behind these bestselling books? How did he come to faith in Jesus? What family life did he have? What did he believe and how did he live? In particular, how did he cope with the difficulties he seemed to face at every turn – a deprived upbringing, a lack of education, poverty and persecution, to name but a few. Bunyan's life coincided with one of the most turbulent periods of British history, a time of civil war and great social upheaval. This might be exciting to read about, but it was not so easy to live through. How

Left:

Copy of
*The Pilgrim's
Progress*

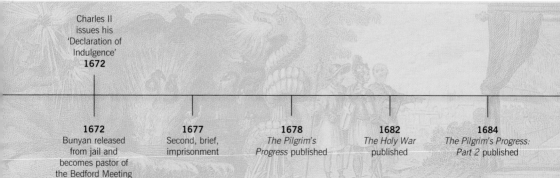

Charles II
issues his
'Declaration of
Indulgence'
1672

| **1672** | **1677** | **1678** | **1682** | **1684** |
| Bunyan released from jail and becomes pastor of the Bedford Meeting | Second, brief, imprisonment | *The Pilgrim's Progress* published | *The Holy War* published | *The Pilgrim's Progress: Part 2* published |

did he manage to survive – and even thrive – in such circumstances? The answers to these questions will show that Bunyan's life, as well as his writings, has much to teach us today.

As should already be clear, I am keen you make connections between Bunyan's experiences and your own pilgrimage with God. In my earlier book on C.H. Spurgeon I included two sections at the end of each chapter – entitled 'Digging deeper' and 'Engage' – to help you to do this. I have adopted a similar approach here, although this time the sections are called 'Going further' and 'Your own journey'; headings which better fit the pilgrim theme. You will get more out of this book if you keep a notebook or journal alongside you so you can write down some of things you discover, and more still if you are able to pray through what you learn as you go along.

So, get ready for what I hope you will find an exciting journey! Bunyan was a champion of the people, someone we can call the 'people's pilgrim'. But he has still been appreciated by Christians from all different classes and backgrounds. Perhaps this is because he was, firstly, focused on Jesus, and secondly, always looking to provide practical help. Percy Dearmer, a nineteenth-century Anglican clergyman, was someone more 'upper class' who appreciated Bunyan. Dearmer adapted some of Bunyan's lines from *The Pilgrim's Progress: Part 2*, for the hymn, 'He who would valiant be'. Some of you – of a certain age – may remember singing it in school assemblies. The hymn begins with the following verse:

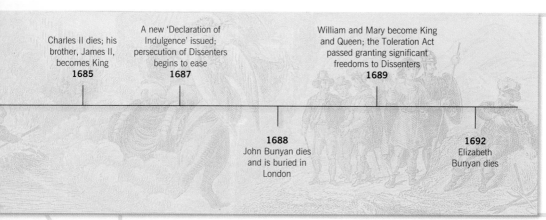

Charles II dies; his brother, James II, becomes King
1685

A new 'Declaration of Indulgence' issued; persecution of Dissenters begins to ease
1687

1688
John Bunyan dies and is buried in London

William and Mary become King and Queen; the Toleration Act passed granting significant freedoms to Dissenters
1689

1692
Elizabeth Bunyan dies

He who would valiant be 'gainst all disaster,
Let him in constancy follow the Master.
There's no discouragement shall make him once relent
His first avowed intent to be a pilgrim.

And ends with ...

Since, Lord, Thou dost defend us with Thy Spirit,
We know we at the end, shall life inherit.
Then fancies flee away! I'll fear not what men say,
I'll labour night and day to be a pilgrim.[1]

My hope and prayer is that you will read the story of John Bunyan and find help for your own pilgrimage. May we all follow Jesus with real 'constancy', strengthened by God's Spirit and so, together with Bunyan himself, inherit eternal life.

Peter J. Morden
Spurgeon's College
February 2012

NOTES

I have worked in the main from 'primary sources' – books and manuscripts from Bunyan's time or soon after. These include Bunyan's published works, the 'church book' of the Bedford congregation of which he was a member, and biographies of him written soon after his death. When I have drawn directly from books and articles written in the twentieth and twenty-first centuries I have included a note at the end of the book giving details.

Bunyan lived in the seventeenth century, and the ways people spoke and wrote were significantly different then. When I have quoted from his books and other seventeenth-century material I have often modernised the punctuation and occasionally the language to make it more understandable for readers today. This has been done without, I hope, changing the sense of Bunyan's original words or the words of his friends.

powere and custody of
chattels, *To have and to hold*
Elizabeth *executors*

John Bunyan
this 23 day of

• CHAPTER 1 •

BACKGROUND AND EARLY EXPERIENCES

Samuel Sanderson

Joshua Symonds

Samuel Hillyard

John Jukes

John Brown

W. Charter Piggott

Ebenezer Chandler

William E. Coates

John Bunyan

Leonard Brooks

Samuel Fenn

C. Bernard Cockett

John Whiteman

Ralph H. Turner

John Burton

Leonard T. Towers

John Gifford

James W. Alexander

✠ TO THE GLORY OF GOD AND IN COMMEMORATION OF ✠
THE TER-CENTENARY OF BUNYAN MEETING (1650-1950)
Evangelist (John Gifford, Minister 1650-55) points the way to Christian (John Bunyan, Minister 1671-88)

EARLY YEARS

John Bunyan was christened as an infant in his home village of Elstow, near Bedford, on 30 November 1628 (his date of birth is not known). His parents, Thomas and Margaret, were not the poorest people in Elstow, but their lives were still very hard. Thomas ground out a living through the trade his son would later take up. His ramshackle tinker's workshop was attached to their house, and it was here he made and mended his simple pots and pans. The home itself, a badly built thatched cottage on the edge of the village, was hardly more sturdy than the workshop. It has long since disappeared, although its site is still marked on many maps. Thomas was almost certainly illiterate: he 'signed' his will with a simple cross rather than a proper signature. For families such as this, life was relentlessly tough. Just surviving from one year to the next was a considerable achievement.

There is no evidence to suggest that either Thomas or Margaret were real Christians. Although they had had their son christened and would have gone regularly to the parish church, this was what everyone did, because in early to mid-seventeenth-century England you risked a heavy fine if you stayed away! Thomas rarely spoke without swearing, and this was a habit his son copied. Much later, when John became a pastor, he would write some guidelines to help Christian children growing up with non-Christian parents. His advice ends with an impassioned prayer, that God might 'convert our poor parents, that they, with us, might be the children of God'. Almost certainly John's childhood experience of life with Thomas and Margaret shaped this later piece of writing.

Not much is known about John Bunyan's early years. As a young child he had frequent nightmares, which he describes as 'fearful dreams' and 'dreadful visions'. He did go to school for a while, learning some basic reading and writing. By his own testimony, as he grew up he also learned 'all manner of vice and ungodliness', becoming the 'ringleader' of the wild and riotous youth of his district. Perhaps he was exaggerating a little when he said this, but he was certainly unruly. He relates one incident which gives us an idea of the sort of boy he was. One day he was out with his companions and saw an adder slithering across a path. The snake does not appear to have threatened him or his friends, but he nevertheless attacked it, striking it with a stick to stun it. Using his stick to force open the adder's mouth, he tore out its poisonous fangs with his bare fingers – a daredevil act that was also very cruel, seeing the snake was still alive. Bunyan said he was 'settled' and 'rooted' in such behaviour, which had become 'second nature' to him.

In his later testimony Bunyan set out his belief God had been watching over him during these years, despite his wayward character and lifestyle. He nearly drowned, not once but twice, the second occasion when he fell out of a boat into the River Ouse running through Bedford. On such occasions he believed God had kept him safe, even though at the time he had been giving very little thought to God.

As a teenager he began to work with his father. As well as spending time in the workshop, tinkers or braziers would have travelled to different villages and towns, setting off in all weathers to peddle their goods wherever there might be a market for them. A seventeenth-century book describes such people as 'strolling tinkers' and travelling 'metal men', who joined other petty traders in hawking their wares from place to place. Like their fellow companions on the road – dealers in poor quality lace and rough linen cloth – these tinkers were often fast-talking and hard-drinking. There is no reason to believe Thomas Bunyan was any different and again, John learnt by example from his father.

Margaret Bunyan died in June 1644 and her eldest daughter, also called Margaret, died a month later. Such early deaths were extremely common among the seventeenth-century rural poor. Diet was bad, disease was rife, proper medical care was non-existent and working life (assuming there was work to be had) was tough – physically demanding with long hours for little reward. Average life expectancy was about forty years, although if you made it out of infancy you might expect to live a little longer. Life for women was especially difficult and many died in childbirth. Despite the fact death was a common feature of village life, the loss of his mother and sister would have hit John hard. Overall, it is quite clear his early years were not easy. Survival was the name of the game and there seemed little hope for a better future.

Left:

The village green with Market Hall, known as 'Moot Hall'

TURBULENT TIMES

To add to the uncertainty and instability, by the time John Bunyan's mother and sister had died, England had been plunged into a bitter civil war. Trouble had been brewing for a number of years. From 1625 onwards there was growing tension between the new king – Charles I – and Parliament. English kings were used to having a vast amount of personal power, and Parliament was increasingly unhappy with this. In 1628, the year Bunyan was born, Charles was forced to accept something called the 'Petition of Right' which set some limits to his authority. But he still tried to rule without reference to the elected MPs. In the country as a whole, those loyal to the king and those loyal to Parliament were increasingly at loggerheads.

Believers' baptism was radical indeed in an age when most accepted the christening of infants without question

This was a dispute about power, but freedom of worship was an important issue too. As far as this is concerned, it's helpful to know some of the background. In the sixteenth century, King Henry VIII had broken from the Roman Catholic Church, and established a separate Church of England (the Anglican Church). The Pope was no longer the head of the Church in England, and some real changes were made to the ways people worshipped. For the first time the Bible was officially available to people in English (previously a Latin version was used in services, which few could understand). Printed English Bibles were openly sold. Those who could read now had access to God's Word in their own language.

Having said there were changes, there were plenty of things that remained the same. There was still only one church. Everyone was to worship in the Church of England, just as before everyone had been Roman Catholic. But there were many, including many ministers, who wanted a more thoroughgoing 'Reformation' in the land. Such people looked to the continent of Europe and what had been happening there for inspiration. 'Puritans' in the Church of England (so-called because they wanted to 'purify' the Church) greatly admired the French theologian John Calvin. They thought his network of churches in Geneva, the city in which he was based, represented a good model. The Puritans wanted to do away with bishops and archbishops and have much simpler worship, with more emphasis on biblical preaching. Such a Reformation had in fact taken place in Scotland where John Knox, who had spent time in Geneva with Calvin, led the changes. At different times in the sixteenth century it seemed as if deeper, more lasting change was on the way. These hopes were dashed, however. In the opening years of the seventeenth century some Puritans thought that a new king, James I (James VI of Scotland), would be sympathetic to them. But he rejected their pleas, strongly supporting the status quo and dealing firmly with any who disagreed with him.

As a result, by the early years of the seventeenth century a significant number of people were breaking away from the Anglican Church and setting up Independent churches. These were not led by bishops, nor did they look to any outside group or person as their ultimate authority. In these new fellowships, the church members would come together to make the key decisions regarding their common life, for example the calling of a pastor. This was not *democracy* (rule by the people), for such congregations insisted Christ was the head of the church (see Col. 1:18). They believed very much in *theocracy* (rule by God), but they also contended all church members could play a part in discerning God's way forward for their fellowship.

The first of these Independent congregations all practised infant baptism, but in the seventeenth century some of these groups, following a close examination of Scripture, began to baptise believers. The first English-speaking Baptist church meeting on English soil was established in 1612, at Spitalfields, which was then just outside London.[2] Believers' baptism was radical indeed in an age when most accepted the christening of infants without question. As the seventeenth century wore on there were further developments.

Increasingly Anglican ministers with Puritan sympathies were finding life difficult in the Church of England. Many who strongly disliked aspects of the Anglican Prayer Book service, and who refused to 'conform' to what was expected of them, were thrown out of the Church. They also established new congregations, swelling the ranks of those who were already outside the Church of England. Some of these were Baptist churches, but there were other types of church established too. The religious map of England was being redrawn. For us today, this seems unremarkable. We are used to there being lots of different denominations and different expressions of church. But in the England of the day this was new, and it created an explosive situation.

Charles I was James I's son. Like his father, he was no friend to those 'Nonconformists' or 'Dissenters' who were worshipping outside the Church of England. He was strongly committed to having one state church, and, what's more, he had little sympathy with the call for more simple worship. His wife, Henrietta Maria, was actually a Roman Catholic and Charles himself liked ritual and ceremony in worship. It seems he wanted to turn the Church of England in a more 'Catholic' direction. Most of the Parliamentarians were either looking to make the Anglican Church considerably more Puritan or were friendly to the new Independent and Baptist churches that were springing up. This contributed to the dispute between king and Parliament. In fact, it set them on a collision course.

Matters came to a head in 1642. Charles had tried to insist the Scots used a modified, more 'Catholic' version of the Church of England Prayer Book. Outraged, the Scots in turn insisted on the freedom of their church. Popular resistance was epitomised by Jenny Geddes, who attended a service at St Giles Cathedral in Edinburgh when the new book was first used. Hearing the unfamiliar and unwelcome words she threw a stool at the minister leading the service, exclaiming, 'False thief, dost thou say Mass in my lug [ear]?' Resentment against the king was at boiling point.

The Scots raised an army against Charles and a small force of

Right:
Portrait of
Charles I
Engraved by
H. Robinson
after the painting
by Sir Anthony
van Dyke

poorly equipped English troops suffered an early defeat against them. The king was alarmed, but for him to raise a proper army he needed more funding, and to get this he had to ask Parliament. They refused to do his bidding. He now had to cope with rebellious English as well as rebellious Scots. The king fled London and 'raised his standard' at Nottingham, formally declaring war on Parliament. The English Civil War – a conflict which also affected Scotland, Wales and Ireland – had begun, and with it one of the most traumatic and lacerating periods of British history, one which split families and communities, pitting neighbour against neighbour and, in some cases brother against brother and father against son.

BUNYAN AND THE CIVIL WAR

As a county, Bedfordshire tended to favour the Parliamentary cause, and young John Bunyan became a foot soldier in the Parliamentary army. It is not clear whether he volunteered or whether he was conscripted – either are possible. As a restless and penniless youth he may have joined of his own accord, perhaps to seek glory and fortune, perhaps to escape his troublesome family life. We do not know for certain. Records simply show that on 30 November 1644, the sixteenth anniversary of his christening, 'John Bunnion' was a private in Lieutenant-Colonel Richard Cokayne's Company of Parliamentary soldiers. It is very likely he had become a soldier a little while before this date, making him just fifteen years old at the time he joined up. For most of his time he was based at Newport Pagnell. This was about thirteen miles from Bedford, but far enough away to make visits home extremely difficult (assuming he wanted to make them). The young man was away from home, separated from the bad influence of his father. But what influence would army life have on him?

Little is known of the military career of this boy soldier, but undoubtedly life would have been tough. All the Bedfordshire troops were short of food, weapons and clothing. Some had to sleep three in a bed. As an example of the lack of clothing, two particular foot soldiers only had one pair of trousers between them. While one man was up and about the other one had to be in bed! There were many months when the troops were not paid and, unsurprisingly, morale was often extremely low. Early in 1645 food was so scarce that some of the starving men mutinied. These were the rather desperate conditions in which John Bunyan had to live. His company do not seem to have seen much action; given their lack of weapons and ammunition this was probably just as well. The Newport Pagnell garrison was never attacked by the Royalists, and so guard duty and training (with what few weapons they had) would have filled most days. Cokayne's troops not only struggled with poverty and hunger, but also boredom.

Bunyan only mentions one specific incident from his time in the army. Writing many years later he says,

> When I was a soldier I, with others, was selected to go to a place to besiege it. But when I was just ready to go, one of the company desired to go instead. When I had consented, he took my place; and coming to the siege, as he stood sentinel, he was shot in the head with a musket bullet and died.

In later life, Bunyan saw this narrow escape as another example of God watching over him in his younger years. There were many ways he could have been killed before he reached the age of twenty. Accidents or battle could easily have ended his life. Disease was perhaps an even greater threat, especially with the dreaded plague sweeping through England, cutting a terrible swathe through the

Right:
Bunyan's house
in Elstow

populations of towns and villages. The fact that he survived into adulthood was for the mature Bunyan a sure sign of the grace of God.

In the early years of the Civil War the king's armies were the more successful. But the Royalists – the 'Cavaliers' – were almost as short of money and supplies as the Parliamentarians – the 'Roundheads' (so-called because of their shorter 'round-headed' haircuts). Thanks to superior military planning and tactics,

particularly from the main Parliamentary commander, Oliver Cromwell, Bunyan's side gradually gained the upper hand. July 2 1644 saw the biggest battle of the whole war at Marston Moor. Cromwell handled his troops skilfully and the battle ended in a victory for the Parliamentary forces, with 4,000 Royalists killed compared to about 300 Parliamentarians. The tide had turned. A year later, on 14 June 1645, the Roundheads won a decisive victory at Naseby. The king fled the battlefield; the Royalist cause was in ruins; the war effectively over.

Charles I was eventually captured, after which he was tried, found guilty and beheaded. The execution took place on 30 January

1649, one of the most famous dates in British history. Cromwell was proclaimed 'Lord Protector' on 16 December 1653, a move that dismayed many Parliamentarians who thought he had become king in all but name. Bunyan's war had finished sometime earlier. Although he had been discharged early in 1647, he had re-enlisted in a regiment due to go to Ireland and fight there. If he had gone, Bunyan's story might have turned out very differently. But there was a change of plan, he never set sail and the regiment he had joined was disbanded on 21 July 1647. So ended Bunyan's rather inglorious military career. If his hopes had been set on adventure or fortune they had certainly been dashed. There was nothing for him to do but return home to Elstow.

Bunyan's time as a soldier was significant in two different ways. Firstly, it gave him some of the ideas he would later use in his books. *The Holy War*, his lively story of spiritual warfare, was especially marked with the military language and imagery he would have learned first-hand during his time as a soldier. Secondly, he was exposed to a range of radical political and religious groups. At Newport Pagnell there were 'Fifth Monarchists', who wanted to establish Christ's kingdom by force, as well as the wonderfully named 'Ranters', 'Levellers' and 'Diggers'. To different degrees these groups advocated political and economic equality, and were revolutionary, often seeking to achieve their aims through violent means. The Parliamentary army was seething with radical ideas, especially so among the ordinary troops. In his garrison hot-headed Private Bunyan would have encountered men who sympathised with all of these different groups, and for a time he was attracted to some of these views.

CIVILIAN LIFE

So, in 1647 Bunyan returned to his village, dishevelled, disillusioned and still poor, and picked up where he had left off, plying his trade as a tinker. Probably sometime in 1649, he got married. One of the difficulties in writing about his early years is the lack of information about key incidents and people. Bunyan himself does not tell us much about his life in Elstow and, although there are some written records from the time which are helpful, they are few and far between. So there are gaps in Bunyan's story. A prime example of this is the name of his first wife. It is possible it was Mary, as this was what the couple decided to call their daughter. It was common for the first daughter of a marriage to be named after the mother (we have already seen John's own mother, Margaret, did this with her daughter). Perhaps John and his new bride followed this custom. Also, the name 'M. Bunyan' was written in the front of a book she probably owned. But to say she was called Mary is no more than an educated guess; no one can be sure. What is certain is that the newlyweds were poor, probably even worse off than Bunyan's parents had been. The young couple didn't have, John says, so much as a spoon or dish to share between them. Their daughter was christened on 20 July 1650 at Elstow Parish Church. Yet sadly, earlier in the pregnancy John's wife had nearly miscarried and although she kept the baby, when the girl was born she was blind. The young couple had been struck early by tragedy.

It is hard to understand what this woman had seen in the wild, impoverished ex-soldier ...

The name of John Bunyan's wife might not be known, but she is very significant to his story, for, although the evidence is scanty, it appears she was a real Christian. Bunyan says that she would often tell him what a godly man her father had been. This father, John was told, 'had lived a strict and holy life' and would not hesitate to 'reprove and correct vice, both in his own house and among his neighbours'. The clear implication from Mrs Bunyan is that she wished her husband were a similar sort of man. John, who wrote about this conversation at a later date, does not record his reaction at the time, but it's unlikely to have been positive! His wife didn't bring any money into the marriage, but she did bring as her dowry two books which had belonged to her father. These were two Puritan works, *The Plain Man's Pathway to Heaven* and *The Practice of Piety*. John had kept up his reading from his schooldays, although up till now he had focused on so-called 'chapbooks'. These were the pulp fiction of their day: cheaply produced and often bawdy stories of romance and adventure sold at markets and fairs. Yet his wife's books were different. The Bunyans would sometimes read them as a couple, probably with John speaking the words out loud to his wife. It is hard to understand what this woman had seen in the wild, impoverished ex-soldier, with his meagre prospects for the future. But she was certainly an influence for good and for God in his life. John did not really appreciate the books they were looking at together, and he still had a very long way to go before he embraced their message. Nevertheless, his willingness to at least read them is a small sign that things were about to change.

GOING FURTHER

In time, John Bunyan, the tinker of Elstow and former Parliamentary soldier, would become a much-loved pastor and one of the greatest writers England has ever produced, a man with a worldwide reputation. However, at this point in his life there was almost nothing to suggest he might be capable of this, or even that he would find a living relationship with Jesus. There was much that counted against him. He had known poverty and hardship all his life and had had a fairly inglorious military career as a poverty-stricken private. He and his young wife had few possessions and even fewer prospects. And now he had a blind daughter to look after. How would he care for his wife and dependent child? As far as Christianity was concerned, in his parents' home swearing and blasphemy had been the norm, rather than prayer and Bible reading. His wife's faith offered a glimmer of hope, but John himself was far from Jesus. As for him being an author, the very thought would have seemed ridiculous. With his lack of education, it appears he struggled to understand the books his wife brought into their marriage. How could he ever produce a book himself? What's more, the few opportunities he had had in life had been thrown away through careless and rebellious living. All things considered, it seemed the travelling tinker was on a low road to nowhere.

Yet John Bunyan did find Jesus and did, astonishingly, become a godly family man, an influential preacher and pastor, and the author of famous books. Ultimately, his circumstances – his difficult upbringing, the death of his mother and sister, his miserable life in the army, his lack of education and the absence of Christian encouragement – did not define who he was or what he would become. When he did offer his life to Jesus, God was able to take him and change him, even healing the pain of his childhood and teenage years. Much of this will be unpacked as the different chapters of this book unfold. But at this point we can already be clear about this: John Bunyan's background and the difficulties of his early years were no bar to God taking him, saving him and using him.

 YOUR JOURNEY

What was true for Bunyan is true for you as well. You may have had to face many disadvantages in life. These might be similar to Bunyan's. Like him, your difficulties could relate to background, class, family, education, conflict or poverty. Or your disadvantages might be different from his. Whatever has happened and whatever the current issues, God can come to you just as you are, bring healing and lead you forward. The difficulties and struggles can be overcome with God's help. Look up the lives of some of the people God saved and used in the Bible. They include people as diverse as Rahab (Josh. 2:1–21; 6:20–25), Jeremiah (Jer. 1:4–19), Simon Peter (Luke 5:1–11; John 13:31–38; 21:15–19) and the Philippian Jailer (Acts 16:22–34). Here are characters who faced all sorts of issues and struggles, to do with their backgrounds, life experiences and personalities. None of them were particularly religious. Yet by God's grace they each found a living relationship with Jesus, and were then used by Him.

Bunyan messed up badly as a youth and it might be that you have done this too, perhaps as a young person or perhaps at some later time in life. Again, this is no barrier to God using you and, again, this principle is clear not only from Bunyan's life but also from the Bible. As I write I have just been asked to speak on Psalm 51 at a meeting which is part of a special week of prayer at our church. The psalm speaks of King David's terrible sin but also of God's love for the sinner who turns back to Him. As David offers himself afresh to God he receives forgiveness. We can turn from our sin, look to Jesus, and God will wipe the slate clean and give us a fresh start. With God, failure is not final.

I hope I am not insensitive to the disadvantages that many people have to battle against in life, and the circumstances which make it difficult for them to fulfil their potential for God. Coming to terms with some of the things that happen to us, and some of the issues we face can be extremely difficult. Neither am I insensitive to people's failings either, partly because I know I have a few of my own! Nevertheless, whatever you have had to face in your life and whatever wrong turns you may have taken, God loves you and he wants to use you, starting from now. This is a simple truth but it is also profound and life changing, one we are about to see illustrated in the life of the wayward and penniless tinker from Elstow.

Samuel Sanderson · Joshua Symonds · Samuel Hillyard · John Jukes · John Brown · W. Charter Piggott · Ebenezer Chandler · William J. Coates

• CHAPTER 2 •

John Bunyan · Leonard Brooks · Samuel Fenn · C. Bernard Cockett · John Whiteman · Ralph H. Turner

CONVICTION AND CONVERSION

John Burton · Leonard T. Towers · John Gifford · James W. Alexander

TO THE GLORY OF GOD AND IN COMMEMORATION OF THE TER-CENTENARY OF BUNYAN MEETING (1650-1950)
Evangelist (John Gifford, Minister 1650-55) points the way to Christian (John Bunyan, Minister 1671-88)

EVANGELIST POINTS THE WAY

Samuel Sanderson
Joshua Symonds
Samuel Hillyard
John Jukes
John Brown
W. Charter Piggott
Ebenezer Chandler
William Cooke
John Bunyan
Leonard Brooks
Samuel Fenn
C. Bernard Cockett
John Whiteman
Ralph H. Turner
THE WRATH TO COME
John Burton
Leonard H. Towers
John Gifford
James W. Alexander

✠ TO THE GLORY OF GOD AND IN COMMEMORATION OF ✠
THE TER-CENTENARY OF BUNYAN MEETING (1650-1950)
Evangelist (John Gifford, Minister 1650-55) points the way to Christian (John Bunyan, Minister 1671-88)

ohn Bunyan came to believe his wife was God's gift to him, and with good reason. He continued to read the two books she had brought to their marriage as her dowry and, as he did so, he discovered a number of things that by his own testimony were 'pleasing' to him. His spiritual search was about to begin in earnest. However, his journey to faith was not an easy one. It took some considerable time and went through a number of different stages.

RELIGION

The first stage of his journey was when he started attending Elstow Parish Church more regularly. He had always been there on a Sunday of course, along with everyone else in the village. But now he started going to services during the week too. As he put it himself, he 'fell in very eagerly with the religion of the times'. Yet, despite this, a whole raft of things in his life did not change. He carried on with his swearing just as before. In fact, his general behaviour was barely altered by this new-found enthusiasm for religion. Certainly he had not found a living relationship with Jesus. Indeed, at this point in his life he did not know what such a relationship might look like, or even that it was important.

The Vicar of Elstow, Christopher Hall, had been at the church since 1639, and would remain there for the rest of his working life, continuing to serve until 1664. During this 25-year period, Anglicanism went through a series of major upheavals and there was much instability. Different versions of the Prayer Book were in use at different times, and a vicar who refused to go along with whatever version was in vogue risked being removed from his parish. Hall remained vicar throughout this period of instability and flux, seemingly without much personal difficulty. This

Left:
Window
in Bunyan
Meeting
showing
'Evangelist'

probably indicates he was not a man of deep conviction. Rather, he was willing to bend whichever way the wind was blowing in order to keep his job. Some of Bedfordshire clergy were devout, godly men, but others were not. A few allowed cruel 'sports' such as cock-fighting and bear-baiting to take place in their church buildings. Less serious, but more comical, was the story of the rector who used to bring his horse into worship with him. Concerned in case someone might steal the animal, he used to tie it up in the chancel during the service, where it was in full view of the congregation![3] Hall does not appear to have behaved like this, although Bunyan does hint his vicar might not have lived an especially holy life.

Hall may not have been known for his personal conviction or his godliness, but he did like ceremony and ritual in services. At this point in his life, such ritual deeply attracted Bunyan. Indeed, he loved observing the actions of the priest, noting the different vestments he wore at different times in the church's year, and fixing his eyes on the resplendent high altar. He faithfully joined in with the said and sung responses. Reflecting back on this period later in life, he believed he had been 'overrun by a spirit of superstition'. Some do find such services deeply meaningful, but for Bunyan they did not open a doorway to a living faith.

Hall did preach one sermon which truly challenged Bunyan. The message was about the sinfulness of playing sport on Sundays. It had not occurred to the young man that such activity might be wrong, indeed it was his regular habit to play games on Elstow village green every Sunday. As Hall preached a real 'fire and brimstone' message on the evils of 'Sabbath sports' Bunyan squirmed a little in his pew, feeling somewhat guilty. His sense of guilt cannot have been that great however, for later that day he was on the green playing sports with his friends despite Hall's thunderous words! The game they were playing on this occasion was called 'tip-cat'. This old English pastime has long since disappeared. It was played with a 'cudgel' (we should imagine something a bit like a rounders bat) and a small piece of wood which was known as a 'cat'. The player would knock the 'cat' straight up in the air. Then, as it came down, they would smash it as far away as they could with the cudgel. The greater the distance the better, as others would have to guess how far it had gone. So, on the Sunday Hall gave the sermon in question, Bunyan was still playing his games as usual. It seemed nothing had changed.

Then, suddenly, something dramatic happened. His mind must have been still troubled by Hall's message for, just as he was about to smash the 'cat' into the distance with a lusty blow, he heard what he described as a voice in his 'soul'. The words were simple: 'Will you leave your sins and go to heaven, or will you have your sins and go to hell?' Looking skywards in alarm, he thought he saw Christ Himself, and imagined He was looking down in judgment. By now the wooden block had fallen to the ground without Bunyan even making a move to strike it. This headstrong young man, who was obviously possessed of great force of personality and physical strength, was terrified. His fellow players must have wondered what was happening. But Bunyan decided to tell them nothing. He returned to the game, playing with the intensity and desperation of a man who had been deeply shaken. This was a significant moment for him, one he could not forget. The phase when he was happy to focus on outward, formal religion was coming to a decisive end. He still knew little of the ways of God, but he certainly was aware of God's judgment. What's more, he was sure religion would not be sufficient to save him.

Left:
Elstow Church

MORALITY

The next stage of Bunyan's journey saw him trying to change his behaviour by his own efforts, a phase I am calling 'Morality'. He tells of another incident which led him down this path. One day, he was standing outside a neighbour's shop, 'cursing and swearing and playing the madman' as usual. The neighbour must have known him well, and she had had enough of his behaviour. She turned on the tinker, telling him in no uncertain terms that his language made her 'tremble'. She had never heard anyone who 'swore and cursed' in the way he did! Bunyan was not used to being rounded on in this way. He might well have responded with another burst of foul-mouthed swearing, but instead he hung his head in shame. If only he could go back to being a child again, so he could learn to speak without these swear words and blasphemies. But now, he thought, the habit had become too ingrained. Real change seemed impossible.

Yet, amazingly, change he did. He was a strong-willed man, 'an all or nothing' type of character who, when he set his mind to something, could often achieve it. To his own surprise, he managed to put a stop to his continual swearing. Encouraged by this surprising success, he started to change in other ways too. He knew the ten commandments, thanks to the Church of England services. He determined to try and live by them. If he had managed to obey the third commandment, 'You shall not misuse the name of the LORD your God ...' (Exod. 20:7), then why not the other nine as well? Bunyan set to work. This was what he described as his period of 'outward reformation'. Once again, this iron-willed man was able to make genuine progress. As a result, three things happened. First of all, those who knew Bunyan were amazed at the difference in him. He became the talk of the village. It was as if he had become a 'new man'. The wild speech and wanton behaviour had gone: now he seemed moral and upright, a paragon of virtue. As Bunyan listened to the praise being heaped upon him, a second thing happened: he became proud. He loved being spoken of as a moral man, loved hearing people say that he was a reformed character. But deep down he knew he had not really changed. He was not keeping the commandments at all, not in his heart. The third thing that happened was that he increasingly began to recognise his failure. Pride was one problem he could not master, and there was much else besides. On the surface everything was well, but he saw the inner reality others did not. He had thought he was making progress, but he came to regard himself as nothing but a 'poor painted hypocrite'. He might look clean on the outside, but inside he was a mess. At this stage Bunyan might not have known 1 Samuel 16:7, but he recognised in his spirit the truth of this verse: while people look at the outward appearance, God looks at the heart. And his heart, he knew, was rotten and sinful.

For some reason, the new 'moral' Bunyan now regarded this pastime as frivolous and 'vain'

In this state, he was troubled once again by thoughts of God's judgment, only this time it was worse. Previously he had enjoyed bellringing. For some reason, the new 'moral' Bunyan now regarded this pastime as frivolous and 'vain'. He stopped ringing the bells at Elstow Parish Church, but here his strong will failed him, because he found he was unable to break away completely. He was so desperate to watch the ringers in action he used to stand inside the church tower so he could see them practice, secretly seething with envy. But after doing this for a while he became afraid again. What if God judged him for watching in this way? He was especially concerned that one of the great heavy bells might fall and crush him. There was a solution though. A sturdy wooden beam ran horizontally across part of the tower. If he made sure he stood under that, then he would be protected. This worked for a while, but Bunyan's imagination was now in overdrive. What if one of the bells came loose and fell in the act of being swung? It might come down at an unusual angle and rebound off the stone wall as it fell. In this way it might still hit him, even if he were standing under the beam! The next time Bunyan watched the bellringing he was doing so from the safety of the door. There at least he would be out of harm's way. But he was still troubled. What if the tower itself collapsed? Miserably, he decided he would have to give up watching the ringers altogether. This all seems slightly amusing, but Bunyan himself was not laughing. His childhood nightmares had returned, more real and more terrifying than ever.

How are we to understand what was happening? To us, bellringing and 'tip-cat' seem harmless, perhaps even a bit dull. Was God really going to judge Bunyan for these things? Perhaps not, but he was right to recognise the seriousness of sin, and the way it separates us from God. Rather than bellringing, his swearing and blasphemies would have been better instances of his sin, together with his inner pride at his moral improvement. Bunyan recognised he was cut off from God and that no outward morality could ever close the gap. His heart was not right and he was powerless to do anything about it. To this extent he had understood his situation correctly.

What he had failed to appreciate, however, was the love God has for sinful people. True, God does judge sin, and it is most important to realise this. But He loves us deeply, as is shown in the life, death and resurrection of Jesus. He longs to take away our sin and share with us His free gift of eternal life. Significantly, when Bunyan is describing his experiences during this period of his life, he rarely mentions Jesus. He was attempting to curry favour with God by living a good life, but he knew little of Jesus and His grace. Largely ignorant of Christ, Bunyan had tried both religion and morality and ended up feeling like a miserable failure, still guilty and still afraid of the judgment of God. But thankfully there was another stage of his journey yet to come.

TRUE FAITH

The events described so far in this chapter probably happened in 1650 and 1651, although Bunyan does not tell us the dates and it is difficult to say for certain. During this period he would

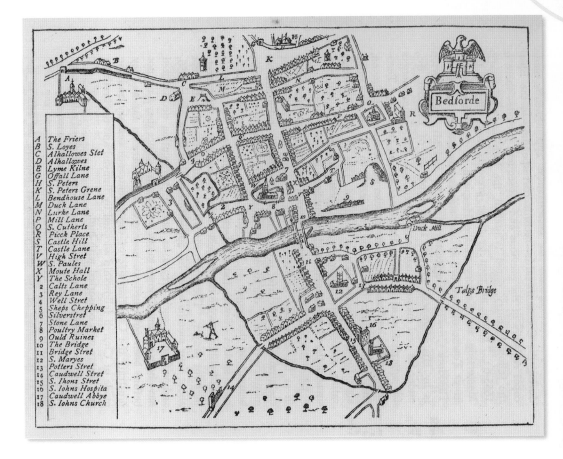

A The Friers
B S. Loyes
C Alhallowes Stet
D Alhallowes
E Lyme Kilne
G Offall Lane
H S. Peters
K S. Peters Grene
L Bendhouse Lane
M Duck Lane
N Lurke Lane
P Mill Lane
Q S. Cutherts
R Pick Place
S Castle Hill
T Castle Lane
V High Stret
W S. Paules
X Moute Hall
Y The Schole
2 Calts Lane
3 Rey Lane
4 Well Stret
5 Sheps Chepping
6 Silverstret
7 Stone Lane
8 Poultry Market
9 Ould Ruines
10 The Bridge
11 Bridge Stret
12 S. Maryes
13 Potters Stret
14 Caudwell Stret
15 S. Ihons Stret
16 S. Iohns Hospita
17 Caudwell Abbye
18 S. Iohns Church

sometimes travel to Bedford to pursue his work as a tinker. In the 1650s Bedford had a population of about 3,000 people. Although small by the standards of today, there would have been many more opportunities for trade there than in the sparsely populated villages and hamlets surrounding the town. On one of these trips something happened that was a real turning point, not for his struggling business but for his whole life. He describes it like this:

In one of the streets of the town, I came where there were three or four poor women sitting at a door in the sun, talking about the things of God …
I drew near to hear what they said, for I was now a brisk talker in matters

of religion. I heard, but I understood not ... for their talk was about a new birth, the work of God on their hearts ... They spoke of how God had visited their souls with his love in the Lord Jesus, and with what words and promises they had been refreshed, comforted and supported against the temptations of the devil.

Bunyan had not heard anything like this before. It seemed that their conversation was 'far above him', as if it had come from another world (in a very real sense of course he was right). And it was not just what they said, but the way they said it. They had a joy and peace of which he could only dream. What was their secret? What was this 'new birth' they were talking about? He was determined to find out.

The women were members of a congregation that met in Bedford. At this point they were small in number, with just a handful of members including the women themselves. He sought this group out and started to attend their meetings. It was one of the new Dissenting or Nonconformist churches that, as we saw in Chapter One, were starting to appear all over England in the seventeenth century. This particular group baptised believers but they were also willing to accept as members those who had been christened as infants. What was vital if you wanted to come into membership was a real and living faith in Christ. This was non-negotiable. All those who wanted to join had to give their 'testimony' to the rest of the group. The church wanted to be as sure as possible that a potential member really knew Jesus as Saviour and Lord. Knowing about Him was not enough, it was vital to know Him personally. It was also important that members had a real commitment to encouraging others in the church. They spoke about 'watching over' each other, and about being mutually accountable. The aim was to have a fellowship that was committed to God and to one another. Here was a different way of doing church.

> *What was vital ... was a real and living faith in Christ. This was non-negotiable*

Their founding pastor was John Gifford, who had an interesting story of his own to tell. Like Bunyan, Gifford had been a soldier in the Civil War. But here the similarities end, for Gifford had been an important officer – on the Royalist side. And, whilst Bunyan had seen little, if any, fighting, Gifford had been in the thick of the action. One battle was particularly significant for it led, indirectly, to his conversion.

This battle was at Maidstone in Kent, a fierce conflict which was one of the most terrible of the whole war. The worst of the fighting took place in the evening as a fearful storm was raging. As darkness fell and the rain lashed down, the Parliamentary forces fought their way across the muddy fields and ditches into the town. When they got there the Royalists struggled bravely in the streets, only slowly giving ground. There was much close-quarter combat as Englishmen grappled desperately with fellow Englishmen. Many on both sides were maimed or killed. Slowly, painfully, the Parliamentarians took the town, street by street and house by house. Eventually both Maidstone and Gifford were captured. Orders were given that this important Royalist Officer was to be carefully guarded. Soon it was decided that for Gifford there could be no mercy. He was condemned to death, with the expectation that his sentence would be carried out quickly. There was no right of appeal for the hapless prisoner. Gifford had just days – perhaps just hours – to live.

What happened next? The Bedford fellowship kept a book so they could record details of their life together. This 'church book' includes the testimony of the man who became their pastor. What we learn is that Gifford's sister came to see him, thankfully reaching him before the execution took place. To her amazement, she found his guards were all asleep! Most likely they were drunk, but the brave woman did not waste time finding out. She urged her brother to take his chance and flee. John Gifford and his sister had just enough time to get clear before the escape was discovered and the alarm was raised. His sister got away but John Gifford himself had to spend three days hiding in a cold, muddy ditch whilst

Parliamentary soldiers scoured the countryside for him. As the search died down, he managed to make his way north to London. Royalist sympathisers sheltered him, but he was still in great danger for he was a significant player in the ongoing Civil War and he was known there. What if someone betrayed him? Gifford needed to be somewhere where he could be more anonymous, and the place he chose to flee to was the town of Bedford.

To begin with, he lived undercover. But, once the war was over and the threat of recapture and death receded, he grew bolder and lived openly in the town. In fact, he lived a wild and dissolute life, regularly getting drunk and gambling his money away. This carried on until one night he lost 15 pounds – an astronomical sum in those days. When he had sobered up enough to realise what had happened he was plunged into despair. He was so desperate that when he came across a book by a Puritan writer – not his normal choice of reading – he picked it up and started flicking through the pages. He discovered the message of Jesus and His willingness to forgive the sins of those who put their faith in Him. Could it be true? Could even John Gifford be forgiven? For a while he refused to accept it and struggled against the gospel message. But his path to conversion was not as long and tortuous as Bunyan's. After an inner battle lasting perhaps a couple of months, Gifford gave his life to Christ. He had experienced a miraculous escape from prison and death, but he came to view his conversion as an even more wonderful miracle, one that had eternal significance.

The new convert sought out some like-minded Christians in Bedford, and happened on a small, informal group who often met together for discussion and prayer. But, rather like the Jerusalem Christians with the apostle Paul in Acts 9:26, these Bedford believers refused to accept that Gifford was truly converted. He was known as one of the wildest men of the town: in fact, he had more than once threatened to kill a Christian who was a prominent member of the group. But eventually he convinced them of the reality of his Christian faith. Gifford was like Paul in other ways

Right:
Stained glass
window at
Bedford Meeting
– John Gifford,
depicted as
'Evangelist' in
The Pilgrim's
Progress, points
the way to
Bunyan, depicted
as 'Christian'

too. The new convert immediately sensed a call to preach and he showed great ability. The small band of Christians decided to come together more formally and chose Gifford as their pastor. There were initially just twelve members. These included the Christian Gifford had once threatened to kill, together with the three or four women that Bunyan had heard talking in the street.

This dynamic group of people whose lives and relationships had been transformed had a dramatic impact on Bunyan. Because Parliament had won the Civil War groups like this could meet freely – for now. As Bunyan attended their simple services he got to know them personally. He said they 'shone' and had the 'seal of heaven' upon them. He was greatly struck with Gifford's effective preaching. He said it provided him with some 'stability' and most of all pointed him consistently to Jesus. Now Bunyan actually heard the gospel, perhaps for the first time. Moreover, it was clear from Gifford it was not enough just to know about Christ and His death on the cross. It was vital to have a personal relationship with Him. Never mind formal religion, did Bunyan have the reality of Christ in his life?  He not only heard Gifford speaking to the whole group, but also spent time with the pastor one-to-one. Many think when Bunyan later wrote *The Pilgrim's Progress* he based the character of 'Evangelist' on Gifford. If so, it was a fitting tribute to the man who was so closely involved in leading him to Christ.

Thanks to Gifford's ministry and the love shown to him by the Bedford church, Bunyan was coming closer and closer to true Christian commitment. He was also helped by his own engagement with the Bible. Indeed, by this time he was reading the Scriptures avidly. He says he was 'never out of the Bible', meditating on its message day and night in order to discover its truth for himself. He thought more and more about his need for forgiveness. Bunyan was drawing near to God, and he began to sense God was drawing near to him.

His conversion probably took place after he heard a particular message about the love of Christ. Bunyan tells it this way. As he made his way home to Elstow after the service, his mind was filled with 'comfort' and 'hope'. Romans 8:39 came into his mind, with its assurance that nothing could separate believers from the love of God in Christ. Now he believed he *could* be forgiven. As he walked along the country track he gave his life to Christ there and then. He could barely contain his joy. 'I thought I could have spoken of God's love and of his mercy to me even to the very crows that sat upon the ploughed fields before me.' The date this occurred is difficult to pin down with certainty – it may have been late 1651 or, more likely, early 1652. But whatever questions there may be about the timing, the reality of the experience is clear. Bunyan had personally discovered the 'new birth' he had first heard about from the women in the Bedford street. He had gone through many struggles before putting his faith in Christ and, as we will see in the next chapter, there would be further struggles to come. But now he had responded to the grace of God a whole new phase of his life had begun. As he walked the road from Bedford to Elstow he was coming home in two senses. He was returning to his home village and he was coming home to God.

GOING FURTHER

Bunyan's experience shows us the vital importance of a real and living faith in Christ. He had tried religion and morality and found they simply did not work. His life only changed on the surface, not deep within, and he had no real peace or joy. Sin was still a problem and Bunyan knew in his heart God would judge this. Then he heard of the possibility of 'new birth' and saw the difference in people who had had this experience. Gradually, he came to see that, through being born again into a personal relationship with Jesus, he could find new life and forgiveness. Only when Bunyan accepted this message by faith did he at last find what he had been looking for.

John Gifford's conversion was in some respects different from Bunyan's. For one thing, it came more quickly. Only a few months passed from the time of Gifford's reading about Christian things to his putting his trust in Christ. But his story also shows us the vital importance of a living faith in Jesus. His life was turned around completely by a personal encounter with the living God, so that he changed from being one of the most openly wild and wasteful characters of the town to being the pastor of the very people he had formerly despised. The Bible talks about the absolute necessity of experiencing the new birth (John 3:1–21) and these two very different characters from history both emphasise and illustrate this vital truth. Morality, formal religion and a thousand and one other things are no substitute for the new birth by which we enter into a personal relationship with God. As Jesus himself says, 'You must be born again' (John 3:7).

 ## YOUR OWN JOURNEY

Your journey with God begins in earnest when you begin a living relationship with Jesus through faith. Of course, God will most likely be dealing with you long before you reach that point. This was Bunyan's experience. Reflecting on his Christian conversion later in life, he saw God had been at work long before he made his commitment to Christ. Examples of this include his marriage and his 'chance' meeting with the women in Bedford. But coming to Christ in true faith was still the vital first step in his journey of discipleship. So it is with all of us. If you don't yet know Jesus personally, you don't have to have such a long and protracted struggle as Bunyan did before you do so. The verses from the New Testament already referred to, John 3:1–21, will help you to 'come home' to Jesus. If you are at all unsure about whether you have done this I would encourage you to read them and believe in Jesus with your whole heart. This is the way to experience the new birth. Bunyan's joy can be your joy too as you trust in Jesus for yourself, and receive eternal life.

And once you have received this, it's great to share the good news with others so they can come home to Jesus too. Bunyan experienced real elation as he realised God loved him. He wanted, as we have seen, to share his new-found faith with the Bedfordshire crows as he walked back to Elstow. Soon he would find some human listeners who would be more receptive to what he had to say! May God give us this wonderful joy and, as we excitedly share our faith, may we also help others to begin their own journey of discipleship.

CHAPTER 3

TRAVELLING THROUGH THE STORM:
Grace Abounding to the Chief of Sinners

Names in surrounding glass panels: Samuel Sanderson · Joshua Symonds · Samuel Hillyard · John Jukes · John Brown · W. Charter Piggott · Ebenezer Chandler · John Bunyan · Samuel Fenn · John Whiteman · John Burton · John Gifford · Leonard Brooks · C. Bernard Cockett · Ralph H. Turner · Leonard T. Towers · James W. Alexander

TO THE GLORY OF GOD AND IN COMMEMORATION OF THE TER-CENTENARY OF BUNYAN MEETING (1650-1950) Evangelist (John Gifford, Minister 1650-55) points the way to Christian (John Bunyan, Minister 1671-88)

Bunnyon.

R. White fec.

Grace Abounding

TO THE

CHIEF

OF

SINNER

OR,

A Brief and Faithful Relation
exceeding Mercy of God in C
to His poor Servant

JOHN BUNY

NAMELY,

In his Taking of him out of the Dung
Converting of him to the Faith
Blessed Son, Jesus Christ.

HERE

Is also particularly shewed, what Sigh
what Trouble he had for Sin; and
various Temptations he hath met
how God hath carried him through

Corrected, and much Enlarged
the Author, for the Benefit
Tempted and Dejected Chr

The Sixth Edition

Cattle and bear, &c. in the Servant
to him for me ;

LONDON,

race Abounding to the Chief of Sinners was not the first book Bunyan published, but it does describe his early experiences, and so here is the most appropriate place for us to consider it. It is one of his most famous books, coming in just behind *The Pilgrim's Progress: Parts 1 and 2* and *The Holy War* in terms of popularity. It was first published in 1666, the year of the Great Fire of London. In some ways *Grace Abounding* makes distressing reading. In the year the streets of London burned, Bunyan published a book which described how he had, in a sense, been through the 'fire' personally.

The book is often described as Bunyan's 'spiritual autobiography', although he only covers the first part of his life. He begins by describing his difficult journey from unbelief to faith in Christ. In fact many of the incidents we looked at in the previous chapter – for example, his rejection of bellringing and his meeting with the women in Bedford – are set out in this first section of *Grace Abounding*. But most of the book is taken up by his relating, in great detail, his struggles to maintain assurance of salvation *after* he had been converted. These struggles began soon after his experience of being 'born again', an event I have tentatively dated as happening in early 1652, and which continued until 1656 or even 1657. During this period of four or five years he was repeatedly besieged by terrible doubts. How could he know that he was really a Christian? What if God didn't love him? Perhaps the gospel wasn't true after all? Or, if it was, perhaps it did not apply to him personally, and so he was still consigned to hell. He went through agonies as he wrestled with such thoughts and questions. Sadly, the assurance he had known when he was bursting to share the gospel with the crows in the fields did not last for long.

For some, this might not be an easy chapter to read. It can be distressing to see a person struggling in this way, not least because it may evoke painful memories of difficult times we ourselves might have faced. Bunyan's thoughts in *Grace Abounding* are often gloomy and inward-looking. He was spiritually depressed and, many writers have suggested, clinically depressed as well. For a number of reasons it is tempting to skate over this arduous period of his life.

Yet I am convinced it is vital to include this chapter. For one thing, it is impossible to write an honest biography of Bunyan if this hard time in his life is glossed over. This is especially so because the

experiences he described in *Grace Abounding* shaped his later life and writings in so many different ways. Also, there is a danger we make out that Christians in the past were perfect – spiritual super-saints who had everything sorted and never put a foot wrong. Again, this is just not truthful. Christians of any era, even great Christians, struggle with all sorts of issues, and they are always flawed characters. Bunyan is no exception. His contemporary Oliver Cromwell once famously asked to be painted 'warts and all': he wanted the artist to portray him accurately rather than flattering him and making him appear more physically attractive than he really was. What I want to do is take a similar approach with this 'pen portrait' of Bunyan, making sure that his temptations, doubts and misunderstandings are not smoothed over or airbrushed out of the picture. This is the pattern the Bible itself gives us, for its characters, even those who are real heroes of the faith, are always described with unsparing honesty.

A 'warts and all' portrayal of Bunyan is not only more honest, it is also more honouring to God, who works through imperfect people so that the glory goes to Him. Finally, it is much more helpful to us personally. Many of us face doubts and temptations and we all misunderstand things and get things wrong at different

Above:

Oliver

Cromwell

times. And we all have difficulties to face and hurdles to overcome. If we read of someone who appears to have had no problems, we easily become discouraged. We are not like them! Reading about real people with real difficulties and how these were worked through is likely to be much more beneficial. So although this might not be an easy chapter, I do believe it is a very important one. Bunyan wanted his open, honest account of his personal battles to become a source of help and healing to others, not least those who, like him, were 'down in despair'. My hope and prayer is that this chapter, which I have called 'Travelling through the storm', will provide similar help today.

DOUBTING GOD

As will already be clear, soon after Bunyan's conversion, his assurance of God's love and mercy vanished. 'Within less than forty days', he says in *Grace Abounding*, 'I began to question all.' To begin with, he lost all sense of God's presence and comfort. It felt as if darkness had suddenly fallen and surrounded him. Such an experience is often called a 'a dark night of the soul', and many faithful Christians have encountered it. Going through a 'dark night experience' can strengthen our faith, for we learn to trust in God and the promises of His Word, rather than rely on our own feelings. Our faith is sharpened; we become more mature believers, better able to press on when the going is difficult. But Bunyan faced additional problems. In particular, he found he was being constantly tempted to blaspheme God's name. This had been his problem in childhood and as an adolescent, but he had been free from it for some time. Now, suddenly, language which dishonoured God started to fill his mind. 'Whole floods of blasphemies' swept over him, he said, causing him 'great confusion and astonishment'. He was used to being overtaken by storms as he walked on the open Bedfordshire roads to ply his trade as a tinker. But now it seemed he was caught up in a great spiritual storm. It was as if the rain was pouring down on his soul and as if his spirit was being blown about by a howling wind. What's more, there seemed to be no shelter in sight.

In this state, Bunyan began to doubt the very existence of God and the truth of the gospel. In *Grace Abounding* he records this battle with unbelief quite openly. What if the Gospels themselves were just made-up stories – fabricated by clever people who wanted to lead others astray? What if the whole Bible was just a 'fable', a 'cunning story'? He tried to conquer these thoughts, turning to the apostle Paul for help. Here was a man who certainly believed, with all his heart, mind and soul. But for Bunyan, this strategy failed. It was no good reading Paul, he reasoned, for the apostle might have been deceived himself. The 'noise and strength and force' of these temptations was almost too much for him and he was coming close to total despair. He felt, he said, like a drowning man.

What if the whole Bible was just a 'fable', a 'cunning story'?

In this state, Bunyan started to find the services of his church almost unbearable. He kept going to the meetings in Bedford, but when he was there he was repeatedly troubled by his blasphemous thoughts. To make matters worse, he felt he was the only one who had problems. He looked around at his fellow Christians and they all seemed to be so happy. They were all rejoicing and 'blessing God', while he was continually caught up in a terrible, swirling 'tempest'. Of course, at least some of these happy worshippers would have been weighed down with serious problems of their own! If you feel the same as Bunyan did, or if you are facing different doubts, questions and challenges, then you are not alone either. Bunyan found this hard to see, and he struggled on in isolation.

Step by difficult step, he was at last able to find a way out of this particular storm. Once again, a text from Romans 8 helped him, this time verse 31, 'If God is for us, who can be against us?' He was also encouraged by meditating on the words of Jesus in John 14:19, 'Because I live, you also will live.' But, according to *Grace Abounding*, the most important verse for him was Colossians 1:20, and the statement that Jesus had made 'peace through his blood, shed on the cross'. Bunyan managed to see that, because of the death of Jesus, he had peace with God. He was also helped by the ministry of the man he calls 'holy Mr. Gifford'. His pastor's biblical, Christ-focused ministry helped him to find some relief. He believed he was coming out of the driving rain and entering a different, sunnier 'season'. He had found help from a range of Bible texts, some good, biblical preaching and, above all, by refocusing his attention on Christ and His cross. But soon he would be in trouble again.

THE UNFORGIVABLE SIN?

The new challenge is described in *Grace Abounding* in distressing detail. As Bunyan puts it, he was tempted to 'exchange Christ for the things of this life'. This theme – striking some sort of pact with the devil and selling your soul in exchange for pleasure in this life – is one that is explored in various books and plays, most famously in Christopher Marlowe's *Dr Faustus*, a play which was well-known in the seventeenth century. Perhaps Bunyan was influenced by this in some way. One morning, as he lay in his bed, he experienced a particularly intense struggle. He was, he says, most 'fiercely assaulted ... to sell and part with Christ'. The words kept running insistently through his mind, 'Sell him, sell him, sell him ...'. He tried to respond, saying, 'No, no'. His chest tightened and he gasped for breath as he made a supreme effort to resist. Bunyan was in the heat of a spiritual battle.

For a split second he wavered and allowed a thought to pass fleetingly through his mind: yes, he would 'let Christ go'. It was only momentary, and it seems as though this thought was not even fully formed. But for him it was enough to throw him into a state of utter misery. He felt that he had indeed sold Christ, and his mood became darker than ever before. His collapse was as sudden as it was great. 'I fell', he laments, 'as a bird that is shot from the top of a tree into great guilt and fearful despair.'

Why did he not confess his sin and receive forgiveness? Bunyan felt he had behaved like Esau selling his birthright (Gen. 25:19–34), doing something which could not be revoked. Moreover, he feared he had committed the sin against the Holy Spirit which Jesus speaks of in Mark 3:29. Jesus says that 'whoever blasphemes against the Holy Spirit will never be forgiven'. This text, taken in isolation, had a dreadful effect on the fragile and overwrought Bunyan. He would never be forgiven! But he had misunderstood the verse. The context shows Jesus was responding to the teachers of the law, who had been saying He was possessed by an evil spirit. If someone believed this and continued to believe it – confusing good with evil and insisting that Jesus was in league with the devil – they would not repent and ask for forgiveness. So it is the *continuing* belief that Jesus is somehow on the side of the devil of which He is speaking. Anyone who is anxious they have committed the unforgivable sin has not committed it, for such anxiety shows the potential for repentance. The key point is that there are no examples in the Bible of anyone asking for God's forgiveness and being refused it.[4] Later in life Bunyan came to understand this very well. But now, because he had thought for a brief moment of 'selling' his Saviour, he somehow felt he had committed this unforgivable sin. Consequently, he believed then he had no way back to God. No one, he says, could know the 'terrors' he went through as he thought about this. He believed he was completely cut off from God and lost forever.

Desperately, he dared to hope he might be mistaken. He longed to know God's mercy, but he was now finding prayer extremely difficult. In *Grace Abounding* he employs the imagery of a storm again, but this time in a different way. Now there was a tempest driving him *away* from God. He was like a boat on the ocean that could not get to safe harbour. He was being tossed 'headlong into despair' and, like a 'broken vessel' holed below the waterline, he was sinking fast. He uses other language and imagery to illustrate his tortured state saying, for example, that he was like a condemned man on his way to execution. His anxiety was so great he developed distressing physical symptoms. He often felt sick and there were times when he thought his breastbone might be about to split in two, so great was the searing pain in his chest. On other occasions he started to physically shake, 'struck into a very great trembling'. Any words of comfort and encouragement from Scripture merely served to torment him further, for he was sure that, although these words certainly applied to others, they were not relevant to him. Verses about forgiveness became a torment in themselves, for he believed they showed him the grace he had lost forever. He was consumed with a sense of overwhelming, crushing guilt and also terrible shame. He did not want to go on living but he was afraid to die.

There is no hard evidence Bunyan shared what he was going through with his pastor. Certainly he does not write about this. Those close to him must have known something was wrong. Gifford was probably aware, but might not have realised the extent of Bunyan's anguish, or the reasons for it. Even his wife may not have known the depth of his suffering. Assuming this was the case, why did he not speak to one of them? His sense of shame may well have held him back, but not sharing his feelings was a serious mistake, as these were people who loved him and who could have helped. Eventually, he plucked up courage to confide in someone, an unnamed older Christian. But he chose his counsellor poorly. When Bunyan told the man he thought he'd committed the sin against the Holy Spirit, the man agreed with him! This would hardly have encouraged Bunyan to talk about what he was going through with any others. He felt exhausted but found sleep difficult. His life seemed to be spiralling downwards.

At last he began to glimpse some hope. A number of Bible verses helped him to see that perhaps he could be forgiven, but still his emotions seesawed up and down. The most helpful text was probably John 6:37 and the words of Jesus, 'and him that cometh to me I will in no wise cast out' (AV). Had Bunyan come to Jesus? Yes he had, many times. So, what did the text say? Jesus would not 'cast out' someone like him. This seemed like good news. (Of course it was, and is!) These words of Jesus began to counteract his fear there was no forgiveness and grace for him. Still he slipped back into his old ways of thinking, often sliding back into despair once again. Nevertheless, his encounter with this verse did help him. Once more, it was through the Bible he was experiencing Jesus and His love.

Finally, one day, as he was sitting with his wife at home, he heard the words in his heart, 'I must go to Jesus.' This sounded good, for it was exactly what he wanted to do! But Bunyan was suspicious. Was there a Bible text containing this phrase, or had he just made it up? He wasn't sure and neither was his wife. Perhaps the words were just a flight of fancy, and not from God. If so, he reasoned, he was deceiving himself if he thought they offered any solid hope. He racked his brains: his Bible knowledge, even at this point in his life, was extraordinary. After a few minutes it came to him. Hebrews 12:24! We can imagine him eagerly reaching for his Bible and flicking through the well-thumbed pages to check and see if he was right. Broadly speaking he was. In Hebrews 12:22–24 the writer reminds Christians they have come 'to Jesus', who is the 'mediator of a new covenant'. As Bunyan drank in the words, did he focus especially on verse 23, with its assurance that the names of Christians 'are written in heaven'? Even if he did not, this was still a turning point for him. Thanks to Jesus there was a new covenant – God had promised free and full forgiveness for all who trusted in Him. Joyfully he said to his wife, 'O now I know! I know!' He had been having ongoing trouble with insomnia, but Christ was 'precious' to his soul that night, and for once he slept soundly. From this point onwards things were significantly better, though it

At last he was at a point where he believed God was merciful ...

will come as no surprise that his struggles with assurance were not entirely over. He draws this section of *Grace Abounding* to a close with the words, 'Blessed be God for having mercy on me.' At last he was at a point where he believed God was merciful, not just to others, but also to him personally. The worst of the storm had passed.

UNDERSTANDING BUNYAN'S EXPERIENCE

How are we to understand what Bunyan was going through? Many have thought that he was suffering from some form of depression. The evidence for this is quite strong. He experienced intense anguish interspersed with occasional bouts of ecstasy, swinging very quickly from one extreme to another. Many of his symptoms, for example his disturbed sleep and his generalised feelings of shame, are indicators of depression. The best academic biography of Bunyan is, in my view, one written by Richard Greaves, entitled *Glimpses of Glory: John Bunyan and English Dissent*. In one of his chapters, Professor Greaves surveys some modern literature on depression, and applies their medical insights to Bunyan's situation. A definite diagnosis is difficult, but his opinion is that Bunyan suffered from something called 'dysphoria'. This involves ongoing feelings of restlessness, tiredness and anxiety, coupled with low self-esteem. He further believes that this dysphoria could have triggered some recurrent bouts of 'dysthimia'. Although it is not the worst form of depression, dysthimia is still extremely serious. Symptoms Professor Greaves highlights include, 'loneliness, despair, emptiness … self-loathing, feelings of inadequacy … a sense of pessimism and hopelessness, and social withdrawal.'[5] Setting this list side-by-side with Bunyan's experience, they appear remarkably similar. In an age when such things were poorly understood, Bunyan appears to have been battling a form of clinical depression.

If we accept Bunyan was clinically depressed, then it sheds important light on his situation. Yet it does not give us the whole story. He also believed he was under *spiritual* attack. As Christians we recognise the reality of this. The Bible speaks of the devil being like a 'roaring lion', going round looking for someone to 'devour' (1 Pet. 5:8), and there are many passages which speak of the spiritual warfare we are engaged in (eg Eph. 6:12). A good biblical balance is important here. It is not helpful to see the devil around every corner and in every circumstance. Sometimes we talk about him too much. The reality is that his power has been broken by Jesus' death so that his final defeat is certain (see, eg Heb. 2:14). Nevertheless, a roaring lion is still a danger, and Christians do need to reckon with him. The man we read about in the pages of *Grace Abounding* was caught up in fierce spiritual warfare.

And there was something else feeding Bunyan's struggles: the way Puritan writers tended to tackle the question of assurance. Up to this point I have spoken very positively about the Puritans. Their writings and example were important to Bunyan, and they can be hugely helpful today too. Many people have found inspiration and strength through reading their works and considering their lives. Bunyan's own writing and attitudes mark him out as being part of the Puritan tradition. But, helpful as they often are, on the question of assurance their thinking needs to be questioned. Many of them thought that Christian assurance – really knowing you belonged to Jesus – was something known by only a few Christians. The Puritan Thomas Brooks, writing in 1645, said that such assurance was 'a pearl that most want, a crown that few wear'. In other words, assurance of salvation was not the birthright of every true Christian, but the preserve of the few. And how was such certainty to be attained? Brooks's answer was that Christians 'must work and sweat and weep'. They must regularly examine themselves, searching for signs they truly belonged to God's 'elect'. Determining whether you really belonged to Jesus could be a long and painful business, with the outcome far from certain.

Grace Abounding shows Bunyan was certainly influenced by this type of thinking. I believe the Bible shows it to be defective. We can find help in 1 John 4:7–21. John wants us to be sure of our

Right:
Title page from
Christopher
Marlowe's
Dr Faustus

salvation. Twice he says, 'we *know*' (vv.13,16) and also insists we can have '*confidence* on the day of judgement' (v.17, emphasis mine). How can he be so sure? Part of the answer is in the love we have for others. This love is evidence God has saved us and is changing us. God has come to us and put His love in our hearts and this love flows out from us to other people (v.19). If someone claims to be a Christian and their lives offer no evidence of this, then those claims have a hollow ring. John also speaks of openly confessing our Christian commitment (v.15). If we declare, publicly, that Jesus is God's Son then that is further evidence that we are really saved (cf. Rom. 10:9). But, whilst it is important to note these things, our love and our public confession of Christ are not the main grounds of assurance, according to 1 John 4. Rather, it is *God's* love and action that is crucial. We are to put our faith in what God has done and to rest in it. In these verses John talks about trusting in the testimony of the apostles as contained in the Bible (v.14), and he assures us God has given us His Spirit (v.13). But most of all he directs us to look to the cross (vv.9–10).

It is what Jesus has accomplished for us there, giving Himself as a sacrifice for our sins, that provides the greatest assurance. Because of this, all those who have put their faith in Jesus can know they are secure in God's love.

Many later evangelicals revered Bunyan, but disagreed with him on the issue of assurance. They had a much more confident view: if someone truly trusted Jesus they could *know* they were really saved. They still sought to examine themselves from time to time, so they could reflect on the progress they were making in the Christian life, and they took sin very seriously. But instead of focusing on themselves, they chose to concentrate first and foremost on Jesus and what He had done for them. Those who took this approach include the eighteenth-century evangelist George Whitefield and the nineteenth-century pastor C.H. Spurgeon. They were well aware they still sinned, but when they did they confessed straightaway and received forgiveness, asking also for strength so they could live differently in the future. Interestingly, it was when Bunyan looked to Jesus, instead of concentrating on his sin and feelings of worthlessness, he found relief. But for years he was unable to maintain this focus on Christ long enough for it to make a lasting difference. If he had been born a century later, and been taught the more evangelical view of assurance, he might have found peace and joy more quickly than he did.[6]

In summary, a number of things combined to cause Bunyan's prolonged despair. One of these was certainly his sensitive temperament, which made him prone to serious bouts of depression. In addition to this, most Christians would accept he was under spiritual attack. But he was also working with a mistaken view of assurance and how this was to be attained. Instead of looking to Jesus (Heb. 12:3) he was looking inside himself, indulging in a lot of introspective soul-searching. The storm he experienced lasted far longer than was necessary. He had doubted, been tempted to abandon God, and then gone through anguish and misery at the thought that God might actually have abandoned him. But at last he had come through, a deliverance that was due only to the amazing, 'abounding' grace of God.

GOING FURTHER

Bunyan experienced some intense battles in these difficult years. He made some serious mistakes, but he also got some things right. Most importantly, he never gave up on God or indeed on God's people, the Church. God and salvation were too important for him to simply walk away. He clung on to God, at times by his fingertips. He reminds me of the Old Testament character Jacob wrestling with the angel and saying 'I will not let you go unless you bless me' (Gen. 32:26).

Yet if Bunyan did not let go of God, of greater significance is the fact God did not let go of him. Sometimes, of course, it seemed to Bunyan that God had abandoned him. He did not *feel* God's presence. But the reality is God never let His child go. And eventually Bunyan did come to see he was secure in Jesus' love. What's more, good came out of even these terrible experiences. We have already seen how Bunyan was helped by different verses from Romans 8. A further verse from this great chapter of God's Word is relevant here. This is Romans 8:28 with its promise that 'in all things God works for the good of those who love him, who have been called according to his purpose'. Thanks to God's grace, Bunyan's struggle for assurance deepened his faith – if he could endure through this he could endure through anything! And it was not only his own faith that was strengthened. He had a new empathy with others in distress, and his struggles helped fashion his ability to write with insight and wisdom about the spiritual life. Indeed we see the truth of Romans 8:28 in action. God worked in 'all things' for the good of those who love Him.

YOUR OWN JOURNEY

Bunyan's experiences can help all of us. I want to highlight a number of things that might be relevant, depending on the person you are and the stage you are at in your own Christian pilgrimage. The first relates to depression. There used to be a huge stigma attached to this in Christian circles. If you were suffering physically, then you could expect empathy, encouragement and practical help. Conversely, if you were suffering from depression, then you could expect to be misunderstood and ignored, with some believing you were less 'spiritual' because of what you were going through. The situation tends to be better now, but it is still far from perfect. If you are experiencing the same sorts of symptoms as Bunyan, then help is available from doctors and counsellors, and hopefully from church too. One encouragement comes from knowing there are others who have gone through something similar to you. Bunyan is truly one of the most influential Christians of all time and there are many faithful believers who have lived before and since the seventeenth century who also suffered in this way, just as there are many who suffer like this today. So if you battle some form of depression then you are in good company. And of course God is with you, just as he was with Bunyan. You are not alone.

The second encouragement is that you can know you belong to Jesus and so have assurance of salvation. I don't want to say much more on this, since it has already been covered at some length in this chapter. But I am convinced that all Christians can know we are secure in Jesus' love. Sin is very serious. Bunyan shows us that. It separates us from God and we need to be forgiven. To recognise the depths of our sinfulness is good, because we appreciate the wonder of God's grace all the more. But sin has been dealt with once and for all at the cross (1 Pet. 3:18). We can know forgiveness and assurance of salvation, not because of what we have done, but thanks to what Jesus has accomplished. What we have to do is trust in Him and His promises (see, for example, John 6:37). My hope is that all Christian believers, by the time they have finished this chapter, will know they are loved by God and that they are secure in that love – eternally.

The third encouragement is not to give up on the Christian life! Once again, comparing our Christian lives to a journey can be really helpful. Sometimes our pilgrimage of faith can be extremely heavy going. As with many journeys, the path ahead is sometimes steep, rocky and narrow. The weather is unpredictable. Sometimes it is sunny, for which we thank God, but at other times the weather closes in. There is rain, mist and a cold, biting wind. It can get very dark. Other pilgrims slip out of sight and the journey becomes

Right:
An early
edition of
Grace Abounding
published in
1688, the year of
Bunyan's death

much more lonely. In addition, it can be hard to see the right path – we may not know which way to go. Managing to keep going when we are being buffeted by the elements in this way is not easy. Bunyan knew this and, of course, later wrote about the twists and turns of true Christian pilgrimage in *The Pilgrim's Progress*. But despite his own difficulties he did 'keep going', even though those difficulties lasted for years. And as he pressed on so his faith was strengthened. If you can persevere through tough times, not giving up on God or God's people, then this is a sign of a strong, maturing faith. And God teaches us new things when our faith journey is a struggle. So, if this is you at the moment, don't give up! Romans 8:28 was true for Bunyan and we can believe it will be true for us as well. As we press on He will work in us, bringing good out of trying circumstances, and enabling us to be a help to others too.

The fourth and final encouragement is that God does not give up on us. If we stumble and fall He picks us up. If we stray onto the wrong path He brings us back. He strengthens us to press ahead. As another wise and godly Christian once said, 'there is no pit so great that he is not greater still'.[7] I think Bunyan would have said a hearty 'amen' to this, and I believe, as we trust God as we walk through the darkness, we will find this to be true for us as well.

race abounding ... *to the chief of Sinners.* 7

preserved me alive: Befides, being in the field with one of s, it chanced that an Adder high-way; fo I having a ftick truck her over the back; and her, I forced open her mouth nd plucked her fting out with which act, had not God been I might, by my defperatenefs, y felf to mine end.

o I have taken notice of, with When I was a Soldier, I, with rawn out to go to fuch a place out when I was juft ready to Company defired to go in my h, when I had confented, he and coming to the Siege...

or fpoon betwixt us both) yet this fhe had for her part, *The Plain Man's Path-way to Heaven*, and *The Practice of Piety*, which her father had left her, when he died. In thefe two books I fhould fometimes read with her, wherein I alfo found fome things that were fomewhat pleafing to me; (but all this while I met with no conviction.) She alfo would be often telling of me, *what a godly man her father was, and how he would reprove and correct vice, both in his houfe, and amongft his neighbours; what a ftrict and holy life he lived in his day, both in word and deed.*

16. Wherefore thefe books, with this relation, though they did not reach my heart, to awaken it about my fad and finful ftate, yet...

Let your Deacons have a constant stock by them, to supply the necessityes of those who are in want: truly brethren there is utterly a fault, among you that are rich especially, in this thing. 'tis not that little which comes from you on the first day of the week that will serve you. I beseech you be not found guilty of this sin any longer So that sowes sparingly will reap sparingly. Be not backward in your gatherings toge- ther: Let none of you willingly stay till part of the meeting be come, especially such as should be examples to ye flock.

One or two things are omitted about your comings together, which I shall here adde. I beseech you forbear sitting in prayer, except parties be any way disabled: 'tis not a posture that suites with the majesty of this ordinance. Would you serve your prince so? In prayer let all self-affected expressions be avoyded, and all vaine repititious. God hath not gifted, I judge, every brother to be a mouth to the Church Let such at have most of the demonstration of ye Spirit, and of power, shut up all your comings together, that ye may go away with your hearts comforted, and quickened. Come together in time, and breake off orderly; for God is a God of order amongst his saints. Let none of you give offence to his brother in indifferent things, but be subject to one another in love.

Be very carefull in gifts you approve of by consent for publick service. Spend much time before the Lord about choosing a pastor; for though I suppose he is before you whom the Lord hath appointed; yet it will be no disadvantage to you, if you walk a yeare or two, as you are before Election. And then (if you be all a- greed) let him be set apart, according to the Scriptures.

Salute the brethren who walke not in fellowship with you, in the same Love, and name of brother, or sister, at that we doe.

Let the promises made to be accomplished in the latter dayes, be often urged before the Lord, in your comings together, and forget not your brethren in bonds. Love him much for the workes sake who labours over you in the word, and doctrine, let no man despise his youth. Muzzle not the mouth of the oxe that treads out the corne to you. Search the scriptures; let some of them be read to you about this thing. If your teacher at any time be laide aside, you ought to meet together as a Church, and build up one another. If the members at such a time will go to a publick ministery; it must first be approved of by the Church.

Finally brethren be all of one minde; walke in love one to another; even as Christ hath loved you, and given himself for you. Search the scriptures for a supply of those things wherein I am wanting. Now the God of Peace who raised up our Lord Jesus Christ from the dead, mul- tiply his peace upon you, and preserve you to his everlasting Kingdome by Je- sus Christ. Stand fast. The Lord is at hand.

That this was written by me, I have set my name to it, in the presence of two of the brethren of the Church.

John Gifford.

CHAPTER 4

MINISTRY BEGINS

Samuel Sanderson
Joshua Symonds
Samuel Hillyard
John Jukes
John Brown
W. Charter Piggott
Ebenezer Chandler
William J. Coates
John Bunyan
Leonard Brooks
Samuel Fenn
C. Bernard Cockett
John Whiteman
Ralph H. Turner
John Burton
Leonard T. Towers
John Gifford
James W. Alexander

✠ TO THE GLORY OF GOD AND IN COMMEMORATION OF ✠
THE TER-CENTENARY OF BUNYAN MEETING (1650–1950)
Evangelist (John Gifford, Minister 1650–55) points the way to Christian (John Bunyan, Minister 1671–88)

ometime in the midst of his turmoil over assurance, Bunyan became a member of his Bedford church. Exactly when this happened is uncertain. According to some notes appended to the seventh edition of *Grace Abounding*, which was published four years after his death, the year he officially joined the church was 1655. But some of the information the anonymous writer of this appendix includes is clearly wrong, so, although it is an important early source for the life of Bunyan, it needs to be handled with special care. In the Bedford church book there is a list of members, beginning with the original twelve who came together in 1650. The entries are not dated, but Bunyan's name is twenty-seventh on the list. This has led some to suggest an earlier date, say, 1653. Because the church was growing steadily, with members joining on a fairly regular basis, this is more likely. What is certain is that, even though Bunyan was going through some desperate inner struggles in the period 1652–57, Gifford and the church were convinced of the reality of his conversion. Consequently, they were happy for him to come into membership.

BAPTISM AND THE LORD'S SUPPER

Bunyan was most likely baptised as a believer at this point. Again there is uncertainty, for surprisingly he never wrote about his own baptism. But the same appendix to *Grace Abounding* states he was baptised when he joined the Bedford church, and this time it is almost certainly right. Later in life he was concerned not to make a big issue of the timing of baptism. He accepted his church's view, that membership should be open to those who had been christened as infants, whether they had later been baptised as believers or not (a position that is known in Baptist churches as 'open membership'). Nevertheless he did believe that believers' baptism was the ideal. Given this, it is hard to think he wouldn't have been baptised himself following his conversion experience. The church's 'baptising place' was in the River Ouse by Duck Mill Lane in Bedford. In the 1650s, under Cromwell's rule, Nonconformists had real freedoms, but services of believers' baptism were still liable to be disrupted by jeering onlookers, who might even throw stones at those who were in the water. So it is possible, perhaps even probable, that Bunyan's baptism happened at night. Ten years earlier he would have been just the sort of person to disrupt a service like this. Now he was being baptised himself.

Despite him saying nothing about his own baptism, he does write about how he started to join in the celebrations of the Lord's Supper – Holy Communion – at the Bedford church. But at this stage he was desperately insecure and mired in doubt, and soon 'fierce and sad temptations' crowded in on him. It was the old problem: he was tempted to blaspheme openly, this time as he waited to receive the bread and wine. He was also afraid that in the past he had not approached Communion with enough 'reverence' (most likely he was remembering some of the times he had attended Holy Communion at Elstow Parish Church). Now he was often afraid as he came to take part. Bunyan's struggles were long and deep.

Nevertheless, as we saw in the last chapter, he came through them. In fact it seems the Lord's Supper played a real part in helping him feel more secure in his faith. The way these services were conducted in the Bedford church was simple and straightforward, significantly different from the involved and elaborate ceremony he had been used to in Elstow. In the uncomplicated and unadorned times of worship at his Bedford church, Bunyan began to see that the words of invitation – 'Take and eat, this is my body which is for you …' – were directly addressed to sinful people such as him. By his own testimony, he came to recognise, he says, that Christ's body had been broken 'for my sins' and 'his precious blood had been shed for my transgressions'. The personal pronoun – 'my' – is most important here. Every person who has turned from sin and put their trust in Jesus can say 'he died for *me*'. The Lord's Supper 'sets forth' this truth with great power. Slowly, painfully, Bunyan began to see this. So the words of Jesus, 'Do this in remembrance of me' (Luke 22:19) became 'precious' to him.

A CALL TO PREACH

Bunyan was still searching for firm assurance when his life took an unexpected turn. Other church members encouraged him to begin preaching. He makes it absolutely clear this call to preach came from them, not him. He felt what he calls his 'weakness and infirmity' and tried to resist. But they kept pressing him, 'entreating' him with 'much earnestness'. Reluctantly he agreed, speaking first of all to small groups in private. It seems strange to think of the man who was going through such inner turmoil standing up and speaking to others. But – again to his surprise – his messages had a dramatic effect. Those who heard him were sure that God had called him to this work and he was urged to use

his gift in more public ways. Bunyan's ministry, a ministry which would eventually have a worldwide impact, had begun.

Before saying more about Bunyan's approach to preaching, we need to record the death of John Gifford, in 1655. Gifford had been the leading figure in the Bedford church from its foundation, and the rabble-rousing ex-Royalist major had become a much respected pastor. His influence on Bunyan had been immense. Unlike Bunyan, who ended up writing enough books to fill a small library, Gifford never wrote for publication. But a letter he penned to the Bedford Meeting whilst on his deathbed was copied into the church book, and this survives. It gives real insight into Gifford's pastoral heart.

As he lay dying he was clearly thinking of his church and not of himself, and his tone is warm and compassionate. He was concerned to remind his people that they had not been following him, their minister, but Christ who was their true Lord. Now more than ever they needed to look to Jesus. Gifford warned them not to squabble over minor issues, for this would threaten their unity. Rather, they should give themselves to prayer and thanksgiving and concentrate on matters which were at the heart of the gospel. He encouraged them to develop the qualities of zeal and love, both for God and for one another. Remaining faithful to Christ and their calling as a church was vitally important in uncertain times. 'Stand fast', he urged them, for 'the Lord is at hand.' The people found the dying Gifford's letter so moving it used to be read to the church at the beginning of every new year, a practice which continued well into the nineteenth century. His ministry as pastor had been relatively short, but because of its quality it had made a deep impression.

Gifford's successor was John Burton, who seems to have been a godly and committed man. But Burton was often unwell and Bunyan, whose reputation as a preacher was growing, sometimes stood in for him. Bunyan also went out into the countryside to preach. Soon, in spite of his own 'great fear and trembling', hundreds were flocking to hear him. As well as experiencing consternation and fear, he felt terribly guilty as well. Who was he, with all his self-doubt and inner turmoil, to preach to others? 'I went myself in chains to preach to them in chains', he said. This was hardly ideal and, what's more, he was being tempted to blaspheme again – now from the pulpit! Thankfully, he managed to resist what would have been a very public disaster, but again and again the temptation came to him. He felt weak and there were periods when he was so anxious he became physically unwell, just as his struggles with assurance led to distressing physical symptoms. Sometimes when preaching he would lose the thread of what he was saying. The strain was beginning to tell.

BUNYAN'S EARLY PREACHING AND WRITING

What did Bunyan preach during this period? By his own admission there was a overriding strong concentration on sin. He was, he says, 'crying out against men's sins, and their fearful state because of them'. It appears he was preaching about sin far more than he was about God's grace. Because he was feeling condemned himself, he had a tendency to stress God's judgment when he was speaking to others. One of the best known quotations from *Grace Abounding* says this, 'I preached what I did feel, what I smartingly did feel'. Because he felt the stinging, 'smarting' pain of sin so keenly, this is what he preached about to others.

His first book, published in 1656, struck a rather harsh note, which fits with this emphasis on sin and judgment. Bunyan was engaging with the 'Quakers' – a group of Christians who, like the Ranters and Levellers, began in the seventeenth century. He disagreed strongly with aspects of Quaker doctrine and practice, for example the view of many seventeenth-century Quakers that Christ was not fully God. The deity of Christ is essential to true Christianity, and Bunyan did well to defend this foundational, non-negotiable truth. But the language he sometimes deployed in the book, which was called *Some Gospel Truths Opened According to the Scriptures*, could be violent. (It should be said that when he was answered by a Quaker, Edward Burrough, the language his opponent used was hardly moderate either!) Bunyan responded with yet another book sharply attacking the Quakers – Burrough, he thundered, was a 'hypocrite', an enemy of the truth who was 'sealed up for destruction'. This was an era in which religious debate was often fiery, and they were arguing about some vital issues. But Bunyan's writing – in content and tone – was quite unlike Gifford's deathbed letter to his church.

This was an era in which religious debate was often fiery ...

As Bunyan became more certain of Jesus' love for him, his preaching did change, and his writing too. As he personally grew in his understanding and appreciation of God's grace, he focused

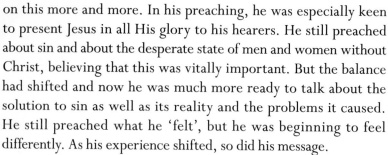

on this more and more. In his preaching, he was especially keen to present Jesus in all His glory to his hearers. He still preached about sin and about the desperate state of men and women without Christ, believing that this was vitally important. But the balance had shifted and now he was much more ready to talk about the solution to sin as well as its reality and the problems it caused. He still preached what he 'felt', but he was beginning to feel differently. As his experience shifted, so did his message.

Bunyan the preacher became more and more effective. Sometimes he felt the power of God to such an extent it was, he says, as if an 'angel of God had stood by at my back to encourage me'. He was particularly keen to preach evangelistically. He implored men and women to come to Christ, and a significant number responded. Bunyan was a passionate man, and when some of those who had made professions of faith didn't continue as Christians he said it was as if one of his own flesh and blood children 'had been going to its grave'. He was committed to the gospel message and to the people to whom he preached. And God was with him.

The Bedford church book records in September 1857 Bunyan was nominated, together with three others, to serve as a deacon of the church. This would have made him one of the key leaders assisting his pastor, especially important seeing that Burton's health was failing fast. But he never took up his role. This was because he was increasingly in demand as a travelling preacher. The church book puts it this way: Bunyan was 'being taken off by the preaching of the gospel'. In other words, he was regularly heading out from Bedford to speak at other meetings in other places. Fulfilling the duties of a deacon alongside this wider ministry was impossible. Many small groups of believers in the villages wanted to hear him, and he went gladly. But his greatest desire was 'to get into the darkest places of the country' and proclaim the gospel to those who did not yet know Jesus.

All this time he continued his work as a tinker so he could support himself and his family. In the Bunyan Museum in Bedford

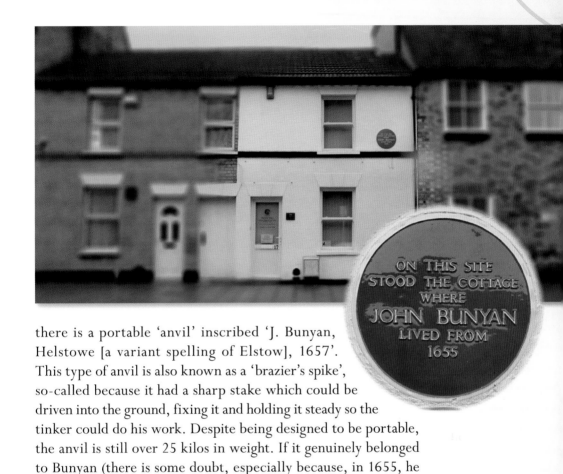

ON THIS SITE
STOOD THE COTTAGE
WHERE
JOHN BUNYAN
LIVED FROM
1655

there is a portable 'anvil' inscribed 'J. Bunyan, Helstowe [a variant spelling of Elstow], 1657'. This type of anvil is also known as a 'brazier's spike', so-called because it had a sharp stake which could be driven into the ground, fixing it and holding it steady so the tinker could do his work. Despite being designed to be portable, the anvil is still over 25 kilos in weight. If it genuinely belonged to Bunyan (there is some doubt, especially because, in 1655, he had probably moved from Elstow to Bedford) it helps illustrate his considerable physical strength. However, although still known as a tinker, he was becoming even better known as a preacher – one with a particular gift for language and the ability to move people's hearts. The tinker's journeys around the county now had a double purpose. Travelling to different villages to ply his trade also gave opportunities to preach.

As his reputation grew, there was a temptation to pride, but he worked hard to overcome it, for he realised this could wreck his ministry. Not everybody welcomed him and he encountered some

Left:
Bunyan's
portable anvil

opposition. Some of this came from those who rather snobbishly disapproved of so-called 'mechanic preachers'. Only properly qualified, university-trained men, they maintained, should preach. A man like Bunyan should just stick to his trade. Undeterred, the travelling preacher determinedly pressed on with his preaching.

Tragically, sometime in 1658 John Bunyan's wife died. By this time they had another daughter, Elizabeth, a sister for Mary, and also two sons, John and Thomas. It does not seem his wife ever formally joined the Bedford church, but in her husband's non-Christian days she had certainly helped him discover Christ, and she has a crucial place in this story. No one knows where she is buried, but those who have been shaped by Bunyan's books and revere his memory owe her a substantial debt. John Bunyan married again in 1659, by which point he was definitely living in Bedford. This time his wife's name is known: Elizabeth. She was a godly woman, one who was particularly brave, as we are going to see. The inner tempest which had so rocked Bunyan, threatening to make a shipwreck of his life, had been replaced by a real measure of peace and calm. However, as 1659 drew to a close, yet another storm was brewing, one which would have severe consequences for him, and for his whole family.

◤ GOING FURTHER

This chapter has covered Bunyan's early ventures into preaching and writing. At this point in his career, it was his preaching which was more significant. Undoubtedly, he was called and gifted. His great strengths, in addition to his way with words, were his commitment to biblical truth and the fact he preached his *experience* of that truth. Bunyan was no dry and dusty academic. To be sure, he thought deeply about things, but he felt deeply too. As already noted, he preached what he 'smartingly did *feel*'.

His passion for evangelistic preaching was particularly strong and he was able to communicate effectively with those who had yet to discover a living relationship with Christ. In his first attempts at preaching, his focus was especially on the nature of sin and its terrible consequences for fallen humanity. But as his approach developed he increasingly emphasised the grace of God. Jesus was waiting to receive all who came to Him in repentance and faith, and Bunyan was determined to point the way. It is important to emphasise he never downplayed what another Puritan writer, Jeremiah Burroughs, described as the 'exceeding sinfulness of sin'. Bunyan continued to speak of this, for he believed if people recognised the depths of their sinfulness they would appreciate the heights of God's mercy and grace all the more. Nevertheless, it was the love of God as shown in Jesus that became his greatest theme.

Initially he was very reluctant to step out and use his gift in preaching. In one sense, there is great merit in this. It shows humility and a willingness to be accountable to others. Those who are hesitant about using their gifts – particularly when this might involve them in some 'up front' role – are less susceptible to pride and more likely to be reliant on God for all they do. Even so, if God has given someone a gift it is important this is used in the service of God and of others. Bunyan puts it like this,

> *I was made to see that the Holy Ghost never intended that men who have gifts and abilities should bury them in the earth, but rather did command and stir up such to the exercise of their gift, and also did commend those that were apt and ready to do so.*

He recognised that if you had a 'talent', God was not pleased if you dug a hole and left it in the ground (Matt. 25:14–30). Rather, that gift was to be used (see, eg 2 Tim. 1:6). Despite some hesitation, this was what he started to do himself. He had had a deep experience of conversion, was at last coming to a peaceful and joyful assurance of faith, and was serving and loving God and others. Bunyan was now well and truly moving on in his journey of faith.

YOUR OWN JOURNEY

As we discover and begin to use our God-given gifts then we also take great steps forward in our own journeys of faith. If one of your gifts happens to be preaching, then Bunyan as he is at the end of this chapter is a good model. His commitment to the Scriptures, his love for people, and his willingness to go to difficult places are all worthy of imitation today. His awareness of the dreadful nature and effects of sin, and his emphasis on the grace of God in Jesus which deals with this, are crucial. Also, Bunyan was never cool or detached about preaching. He knew it was a serious business, for he was standing before people who desperately needed to hear and respond to the gospel message. Utterly convinced of this, he threw himself into his work, body and soul.

Yet, of course, your gifts and abilities may be very different to his. You may have a fair idea of what these are already, or you may be unsure. As you begin to discover how God has gifted and called you, you might be hesitant about using your 'talent'. This is good, as long as it leads you to rely on God all the more. But don't bury your talent in the ground. There comes a time when we have to recognise God calls us to use our gifts, and once we have recognised this, to take action. As the saying goes, we are 'saved to serve'.

This is a crucial dimension of our Christian pilgrimage. For we make progress not just by sitting and receiving, but by getting up and getting involved. As we actively live for God He shows us far more than would be the case if we were merely passive. As Bunyan began to exercise his gift his 'spiritual muscles' grew stronger. If we want to press on in our own journeys with God, one of the surest ways to do this is to serve. May we listen to the encouragement Bunyan gives us, and 'stir up' and 'exercise' our gifts in the service of God and of others.

Samuel Sanderson

Joshua Symonds

Samuel Hillyard

John Jukes

John Brown

W. Charter Piggott

Ebenezer Chandler

William J. Coates

John Bunyan

Leonard Brooks

Samuel Fenn

C. Bernard Cockett

John Whiteman

Ralph H. Turner

John Burton

Leonard J. Towers

John Gifford

James W. Alexander

ARREST, TRIAL AND IMPRISONMENT

✠ TO THE GLORY OF GOD AND IN COMMEMORATION OF ✠
THE TER-CENTENARY OF BUNYAN MEETING (1650–1950)
Evangelist (John Gifford, Minister 1650–55) points the way to Christian (John Bunyan, Minister 1671–88)

In 1659, at the age of thirty-one, Bunyan had already experienced many things. There had been much sadness and struggle. He had been a rebellious youth and had risked death by becoming an infantryman in the Civil War. He had seen his first child born blind and then, later, his first wife die, leaving him with four dependent children. He had become a Christian only after a prolonged period of confusion and difficulty and had then gone through agonies of doubt as he desperately sought assurance God really loved him. He had known periods of deep depression. But there was also much that was positive, a significant amount of which had grown out of these tough periods. He now had a strong trust in Jesus and a burning desire to follow Him – in the church and in the wider world. He had taken his first steps as a writer. He was also an effective preacher, one who was able to communicate the Christian faith in a clear, lively and engaging way to ordinary people. Partly because of the hard times he had known, he had great sympathy and love for those who experienced life as a struggle. This compassion for people, allied with his passion for Jesus and his way with words, made him a sought after speaker. Now remarried, the immediate future seemed bright for this in-demand 'mechanic preacher'.

THE MONARCHY RESTORED

The political situation was beginning to change however. The year Bunyan's first wife died – 1658 – also saw the death of Oliver Cromwell, the Lord Protector. Cromwell's third son, Richard, was his father's chosen successor. But he was distrusted by the army, having never fought in the Civil War, and many in Parliament disliked him too. Richard Cromwell has often been caricatured as a weak leader who was never up to the job. Yet he faced a

Left:
Scene from
*The Pilgrim's
Progress*

deteriorating set of circumstances which would have severely tested anyone. His 'reign' as Lord Protector was ineffective and brief, lasting just nine months. After this, Parliament and the army were increasingly at loggerheads. The country seemed leaderless and rudderless, with no clear direction being set. The Puritan Commonwealth upon which Nonconformists had set such high hopes was collapsing.

A new Parliament was called, meeting for the first time in April 1660. What were they to do? This Parliament was far more Royalist than previous ones and, given the rather chaotic and dangerous situation they faced, they took a momentous decision: they would return the king to his throne. In fact, this Parliament proclaimed that the son of the executed Charles I had in fact been the rightful ruler of England ever since the execution of his father! It wasn't so much turning back the clock: rather, it was as if the last thirteen years of Civil War and Republican government had never happened. The Puritan Commonwealth was being written off as a gigantic mistake. Charles Stuart – Charles II as he was to be known – had been in exile in Europe, hoping one day to return and claim his father's crown. That moment had now arrived. He arrived in London to great fanfare on 29 May 1660, a day which happened to be his birthday and which was later made an annual public holiday in his honour. England's Republican experiment was over.

There is no doubt that some rejoiced at the restoration of the monarchy. But many others were unhappy, despite the fact there seemed no obvious viable alternative. And some were deeply

Above:
Site of
Bunyan's
arrest

concerned, Nonconformists among them. What would this mean for religious freedom? In the days of the Republic, Dissenters had been able to worship freely. Bunyan's congregation had actually been meeting in St John's Church in Bedford, holding their own services in the building when the parish church was not using it. Charles had promised, were he to become king, none of his subjects would suffer due to their 'opinions or religious beliefs' as long as they lived 'peaceably'. Would this promise be kept? Would Bunyan's Bedford church be able to continue worshipping in peace? They were soon to find out.

Bunyan was one of those who could not escape a sense of foreboding: 'I saw what was a-coming', he said. Under Charles II, Anglicanism in England was fully restored, along with its system of bishops and archbishops, and the Church of Scotland had to accept this too, something it did with great reluctance. In 1660 Bunyan's Bedford congregation lost the use of St John's Church and had to return to meeting in private homes. This was also the year their ailing pastor, John Burton, finally succumbed to illness and died. The church was now without a pastor and without a building to meet in. John Gifford's call to his church to 'stand fast' in difficult times, given in his last letter to them, was turning out to be prophetic and necessary. In Bedfordshire, conformity to Anglicanism was strictly enforced – all were meant to attend their parish church. A travelling tinker who would not accept this, and who refused to stop preaching at what were now illegal meetings, was likely to encounter serious trouble.

In Bedfordshire, conformity to Anglicanism was strictly enforced …

BUNYAN'S ARREST AND TRIAL

And so it proved. As we saw in the Introduction, Bunyan was arrested at Lower Samsell on 12 November 1660, as he was about to preach Christ to the people there. The charge against him accused him of failing to attend his local Anglican church and, most seriously, with preaching at 'several unlawful meetings … to the great disturbance and distraction of the good subjects of this Kingdom'. Bunyan was a champion of the poor but he was not a political revolutionary. On the very day he was arrested his Bedford church was holding a day of prayer for the country's rulers. As far as he himself was concerned, this former parliamentary soldier had already professed loyalty to the new king as long as this did not conflict with his greater loyalty to God, saying, 'I look upon it as my duty to behave myself under the king's government, both as becomes a man and a Christian.' But this was to no avail. Preaching to a Congregational or Baptist meeting was now considered subversive activity. Some 'unlicensed' preachers managed to avoid arrest, but Bunyan's popularity counted against him. After his arrest, he was most likely held for the night at Harlington House, just to the south of Lower Samsell. Tradition has it he slept in a room at the top of the house which became known as 'Bunyan's cell'. The following day he appeared before the local authorities, with his main interrogator being Francis Wingate, the rich owner of Harlington House. Wingate was a local Justice of the Peace, an ardent Royalist and staunchly opposed to Nonconformists. There seemed no way out.

Still, there was a way of escape which, on one level, would have been quite easy to take. If Bunyan had agreed to stop preaching he could have been released. But he steadfastly refused. The authorities insisted he should 'follow his calling', by which they meant that he should stick to his trade as a tinker. But Bunyan believed he now had another calling – to preach. He could not be silent without being disobedient to God. He resolved to remain faithful to this, whatever the cost. In a prison cell awaiting trial he wrote,

Right:
Stone set into pavement on the site of Bedford County Jail

Here I lie waiting the good will of God to do with me as he pleaseth, knowing that not one hair of my head can fall to the ground without the will of my Father who is in heaven. Let the rage and malice of men be what

they may, they can do no more and go no further than God permits them; and even when they have done their worst, we know that all things work together for good for them that love God.

Bunyan was sure of two things: firstly, that God was sovereign and, secondly, that God, his heavenly Father, cared for him. Once again, Romans 8:28 was relevant, as he trusted that God would somehow work in this situation for good. Viewed from our perspective, we can see this is exactly what happened. God was as good as His word. But for Bunyan to affirm this in his dark, cold cell needed great faith. Are we able to walk by faith and not by sight (2 Cor. 5:7), trusting in God and His promises in the dark as well as in the light?

At Bunyan's trial, which took place in January 1661, he argued passionately with the assembled magistrates who met under the chairmanship of Sir John Kelynge, another man who was no friend to Nonconformists. Bunyan quoted numerous Scriptures to support his case – he certainly knew the Bible much better than Kelynge and the other magistrates did. (Bizarrely, Kelynge said the Anglican Prayer Book had been around since the time of the Apostles!) But Bunyan's Bible knowledge counted for little as far as the court was concerned.

There was never much doubt he would be found guilty, particularly as Kelynge was effectively both judge and jury. To be fair, as the law of the land stood, Bunyan was guilty. He was sent to jail, initially for three months. If, at the end of this period, he would agree to attend the Church of England and give up his preaching, he could expect to be released. But if he refused then he was likely to be banished from the country, 'transported' on a long, dangerous sea voyage to the Caribbean or America. If he survived the journey (and many did not) he would most likely be put to work as a slave. Furthermore, if he ever returned to his native land without the express permission of the king, then he would be

hunted down and hanged, dying the death of a common criminal. Bunyan's farewell words to the court were brave indeed. 'If I were out of prison today,' he declared, 'I would preach the gospel again tomorrow, by the help of God.' With this dramatic pronouncement, Bunyan was led away to jail. The situation looked bleak indeed.

IMPRISONMENT

Whilst all this was happening, his wife and family were in a desperate state. On hearing the news of her husband's arrest, Elizabeth, who was pregnant, went into premature labour. Tragically, her baby died. She now faced a future every bit as uncertain as her husband's. She had her four dependent step-children to care for, and no source of income. John had been brave at his trial, but he was not insensitive to the situation faced by his wife and family. From his own point of view, he missed them terribly. Being parted from them was like having the flesh torn from his bones. With regard to their future, he felt as if he was 'pulling down his house upon the head of his wife and children'. Miserably, he pictured them facing all kinds of 'hardships' and 'wants'. He was especially concerned for his 'poor, blind child', Mary. In his mind's eye he played out a variety of different scenarios as he thought of what her future might be. He could picture her starving and begging in the street, perhaps in rags, perhaps even naked. She might also be beaten and suffer a thousand other nameless 'calamities'. He believed he was doing the right thing in taking his stand, 'I must do it, I must do it', he declared. Yet even as he resolved to be faithful to what he believed Christ was saying, he was in torment, feeling as if his heart would break into pieces at any moment.

Within the four walls of the jail, there was very little John Bunyan could do to bring about his release. But with resourcefulness and bravery, Elizabeth took up the challenge. Sometime after April 1661 she travelled to London to try to gain her husband's freedom. If perseverance and courage had been enough, she would have succeeded. She appealed to a member of the House of Lords whom she hoped would be sympathetic, and then took her case before one of the London courts. At one point she daringly threw a written petition into the coach of a judge in the hope of getting him to consider the case. Again and again, she attempted to get the decision overturned. As a last resort she went to the Swan Inn in Bedford, where several judges were meeting together. With amazing boldness for a seventeenth-century woman faced with such a situation, she entered the inn, confronted the judges, and courageously put the case for her husband's innocence.

John Bunyan himself wrote admiringly of his wife's attempts to get his conviction overturned. His short work, *The Relation of the Imprisonment of Mr John Bunyan*, which is attached to many of the later editions of *Grace Abounding*, includes an account of the meeting at the Swan Inn, as told to him by his wife. According to this, Elizabeth tried every argument she could think of to persuade the startled judges. She appealed to the law (although in reality the unjust law of the land was not on her side) and insisted her husband wanted to live peaceably. Some of the judges were sympathetic, but others were not. One of the more hostile called her tinker/preacher husband a 'pestilent fellow' and stubbornly refused to listen. Another declared

Left:

Door in county jail – probably to prisoners' day room

that if her husband would 'leave preaching' the situation would change. Elizabeth retorted that he dare not leave preaching; as long as he was able to speak he would continue to use his gift. She asked them to consider her situation and that of her family: 'I have four small [step] children, that cannot help themselves, of which one is blind, and have nothing to live upon, but the charity of good people.' By now it seems she had the attention of the assembled group. It must have been a highly charged, dramatic scene. But this appeal to their pity failed too. As it became clear there was little hope of reprieve she cried out, 'Because he is a tinker and a poor man therefore he is despised, he cannot have justice.' It was a magnificent ending to her attempt to gain Bunyan's release, one which was probably doomed to failure even before it started. Faithful Elizabeth Bunyan left in tears; John Bunyan remained in prison. Only one 'concession' was given. Because of the faint possibility he might ask for a pardon and agree to give up preaching, he was not after all deported from the country. Instead, he would spend most of his time from 1660 to 1672 languishing in prison.

INSIDE BEDFORD JAIL

What were conditions like for Bunyan? Seventeenth-century English jails were grim places, and Bedford County Jail was no exception. (There is a tradition Bunyan was held in the tiny jail which used to stand on Bedford Bridge. But this is almost certainly wrong, although he probably spent some time in this smaller lock-up later in life.[8]) Bedford County Jail stood on the corner of the High Street and what today is called Silver Street. It was demolished in 1801 and no painting or sketch of it survives. However, a written description produced when the building was still standing says it had two floors, some dungeons below ground and a small courtyard for prisoners to exercise in. The prisoners' cells had no fireplaces, and so they would have been bitterly cold in winter. There were hardly any furnishings, with no proper beds (the prisoners might

– if they were fortunate – have some straw to sleep on). There is some hint of the desperate conditions inside Bedford County Jail in a letter from a prisoner, John Bubb, sent to the king in 1666. Bubb had been in prison for a year and was pleading for release. He said the jail was a 'dismal place' and that he himself was in a 'calamitous condition', likely to perish unless the king had mercy on him. Bubb had seriously wounded a man in a drunken brawl (a month after the fight, the man in question died). Nevertheless, fairly soon after his letter to the king, he was released. Bubb's fellow prisoner, Bunyan, whose only 'crime' was preaching the gospel, had no such reprieve. A door from the prison is preserved at the Bunyan Museum. It is large and imposing, fastened with iron bolts and with a small opening in the centre which is itself protected by bars so that no one could escape through it. Behind this heavy oak door John Bunyan was destined to spend a significant part of his life.

GOING FURTHER

Bunyan was determined to remain faithful to his principles and his calling. He believed Christians should be able to meet freely, and he believed he was gifted and called as a preacher, a calling

which had been affirmed by other believers. Because of these unshakable convictions, and his commitment to act upon them, he was imprisoned. In many ways, in his early thirties he was at the height of his powers – physically strong and growing in Christian maturity and fruitfulness. But with this new turn of events he was to spend the next twelve years – time that he would otherwise have spent in preaching, witnessing, church work, and enjoying family life – behind bars, held in conditions many of us today find hard to imagine. He had not done anything wrong; he had merely sought to remain true to God.

Faithfulness to God and the gospel does not always mean that things are easy for us in this life. In fact it may mean exactly the opposite! Bunyan's commitment to follow Jesus had led him into a difficult place. This is a sobering thought for many of us who live rather comfortable lives, but it is nothing less than biblical Christianity (see, for example, Luke 9:23; John 21:18–19). Bunyan and many other Christians would have agreed with the sentiments expressed in the well-known nineteenth-century hymn:

> *Father, hear the prayer we offer:*
> *Not for ease that prayer shall be,*
> *But for strength, that we may ever*
> *Live our lives courageously.*[9]

This was Bunyan's approach, and that of his wife Elizabeth. Both lived faithfully and with great courage; both suffered as a result of their principles and desire to follow Jesus. Their examples are a challenge to Christians – especially Western Christians – today.

YOUR OWN JOURNEY

Bunyan was being persecuted for his faith. He suffered loss of freedom, separation from family, and much else besides because he was determined to remain faithful to God and exercise his gift of preaching. When we are similarly faithful, we are going to come up against opposition too. In 2 Timothy 3:12 it says, 'Everyone who wants to live a godly life in Christ Jesus will be persecuted.' We need to take this powerful verse seriously. If we take it at face value, it tells us that if we are never persecuted for our faith then we cannot be living sufficiently godly lives! In emphasising this, I am not suggesting we seek out persecution, still less that we attract it by being deliberately contentious or unwise in our witness. Our desire should simply be to live a 'godly life in Christ Jesus', that is to follow Christ wholeheartedly in every area of our lives. If we do this some will be attracted to us, and we will know great joy and live a life of real fruitfulness. But some will be repelled by our faith and we will face some persecution, sooner or later. Bunyan's life illustrates this clearly. We need to be ready to face opposition, and when the time comes we need to follow Gifford's advice, and Bunyan's example, and 'stand fast'.

Yet the reality is Bunyan lived in especially difficult times, when being a Christian with principles and a desire to be all out for God was particularly hard. The majority of us in the West today do not have to live in such a context, at least at the moment. I write as a British pastor and, although it is certainly not easy to follow Jesus in Britain today, we are not persecuted in the way Bunyan was. There are believers in other parts of the world, however, for whom state persecution is very real. Some of the words and phrases from this chapter – for example, 'unlicensed meeting', 'arrest', 'trial' and 'prison' – are all too familiar to Christians brothers and sisters around the world, not as words on a page but as actual and present realities. Indeed, there are many who face worse than even Bunyan experienced, not only imprisonment and threat of banishment but actual torture and death. We need to remember these friends. In this book we are talking about our own journey of faith, but as we make progress in this we realise a significant part of Christian discipleship is to do with supporting others. So we should be encouraged to pray for the Persecuted Church and to support Christians who suffer greatly because they follow Christ. There are some excellent organisations to help us do this.[10] Two questions, then, for us to consider at the close of this chapter: will we be faithful to God's calling on our lives whatever it costs us? And will we pray and support others who are paying a high price for doing the same?

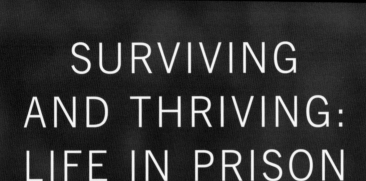

SURVIVING AND THRIVING: LIFE IN PRISON

ON A CERTAIN PLACE WHERE WHERE WAS A DEN AND LAID LIGHTED ME DOWN WORLD IN THAT OF THIS PLACE TO WILDERNESS THE SLEEP AND THROUGH AS I SLEPT WALKED I DREAMED AS I A DREAM

IN COMMEMORATION OF THE TERCENTENARY OF THE PUBLICATION OF THE PILGRIMS PROGRESS ON THE 18th FEBRUARY 1678.

This chapter says a little more about Bunyan's life in Bedford Jail. In particular it looks at the question, 'How did he both survive *and* thrive in prison?' To think of him *thriving* in such a situation seems especially strange. Surely this is the wrong word to use? Jail – especially a seventeenth-century English jail – could be a place of terrible hardship. Bunyan's home for nearly twelve years was a dank, dirty, overcrowded prison. He had lost his freedom and was separated from his family, and so was unable to care for them. The threat of banishment and death hung over him. Surviving would be hard enough: how could he possibly flourish in such circumstances? Nevertheless, it really is true to say Bunyan spiritually prospered in prison. How this happened is the subject of this chapter.

PHYSICAL SURVIVAL

Physical survival was clearly an immediate concern. This was by no means easy. The prison food was woefully inadequate, and prisoners were somehow expected to find a way of supplementing it. His family sought to provide help, with Mary learning the route to the prison by heart so she could bring him some soup in a little jug. Bedford County Jail had a number of small, heavily barred windows which opened out on to Silver Street, and prisoners used to push their hands through the bars to plead for aid from passers-by. Although it seems unlikely Bunyan would have begged like this, it was probably through one of these windows that Mary passed the soup to her father. In this and in other ways, his family, although they were in a precarious position themselves, sought to help him. His Bedford church would have been active in giving aid as well. They were almost certainly the 'good people' Elizabeth had referred to when she was talking to the judges at the Swan Inn, those whose 'charity' she was relying on. But there were times when some of these church members were imprisoned themselves, and even if they avoided jail, they could be hit with crippling fines for failing to conform to Anglican worship. In these circumstances, Bunyan did what he could to support himself. He made countless 'tagged laces' — laces which could be used in shoes and for other purposes. These were then sold for a pittance. John Bunyan and all except one of his family managed to survive but, particularly in the early years when he received very little income from his writing, it must have been a close run thing.

The family member who did not live to see her father's eventual release was Mary, who died in 1663. Mercifully, Bunyan's worst fears — that his blind daughter would become destitute, beaten and abused by others — do not appear to have been realised. The precise cause of her death is not known. But probably she caught one of the dangerous diseases all too prevalent in the England of the day and did not have the physical strength to fight it off. Bunyan was stricken with grief. Following her death he wrote a short treatise entitled the *The Resurrection of the Dead*. In his sadness he comforted himself with the thought that in Christ his daughter was safe and that, one day, she would rise again. In his dark, lonely prison cell, Bunyan sought to put his trust in God for a better future, not only for himself but also for his dearly loved daughter. But Mary's death was still a bitter blow.

It is important not to paint too desperate a picture of Bunyan's imprisonment. He was allowed a Bible and another book called *Foxe's Book of Martyrs*, and clearly he had access to writing materials. He also had a sympathetic jailer who would occasionally let him out of the prison, as long as he promised to return! This happened on a regular basis during a six-month period from autumn 1661 to spring 1662. The prisoner was allowed to visit his family at home and also preach at his church and in other places in the Bedford area. He even made a trip to London and preached there. But when the authorities heard about this they were furious, both with

Right:
Latimer and Ridley being burned at the stake from a plate from *Foxe's Book of Martyrs*

the jailer (who was almost dragged before the court himself) and with Bunyan. They accused Bunyan of going to London to plot a political insurrection against the state. This, the prisoner insisted, was a nonsense and a 'slander'. Rather, he had gone to encourage Christians and to proclaim the Word of God. But the authorities were unmoved. As can be imagined, there followed a period when Bunyan was closely guarded indeed. As his imprisonment unfolded there were other periods when he was occasionally allowed out. In 1666, when the Plague threatened to sweep through the jail, he was mercifully sent home for a short time. Nevertheless, the norm for Bunyan was close confinement in conditions that would be regarded as totally unacceptable in Britain today.

It is little surprise that in such circumstances his depression returned. In *A Brief Account of the Author's Imprisonment* he speaks of being in a 'very sad and low condition' at a time when he was a 'young prisoner'. Probably this was sometime in 1663 or 1664. This was after Mary's death and when hopes of his own early release were fading. He had been shaken to the core by the loss of his daughter and had become afraid, he said, that his imprisonment 'might end at the gallows'. But there was an even greater fear. What if he were tortured and, finding it too much to bear, denied his Lord? *Foxe's Book of Martyrs* was full of stories of Protestant believers who, at the time of the sixteenth-century Reformation, had been killed because of their faith. They had often died heroically, refusing to deny Christ as they were burned at the stake, even managing to speak words of gospel encouragement to the gathered crowd. Would Bunyan be able to show the same courage and resolution? He was not so sure. As he wrestled with these fears he turned to God for comfort. But for a while God seemed distant, as had been the case during Bunyan's earlier struggles with assurance. Indeed, he felt that the 'things of God were hid from [his] soul'. In the bleak confines of the jail, it seemed his doubts and inner uncertainties were returning to haunt him again. But this time his depression passed more quickly. He found he was strengthened, firstly through the Scriptures and secondly through prayer.

THE BIBLE

In jail, Bunyan delved into his Bible again and again. There were particular passages that, he says, were a 'great refreshment' to him. One of these was John 14:1–4. In these verses Jesus reassures His disciples, frightened at the thought of Jesus 'going away'. Specifically, He insists there are 'many rooms' in His 'Father's house', and that He is going ahead of them to 'prepare a place' for them. This Scripture was a tremendous encouragement to Bunyan. He put his trust in Jesus' promise and as he did so, he found his nerve steadied. He came to appreciate the wonder of his salvation in a fresh way. 'I have had sweet sights of my forgiveness of sins in this place', he wrote, 'and of my being with Jesus in another world.' His fears of death and of denying Christ receded. Whatever happened, he knew he was safe in God's care. Even if death came, he had a sure and certain future to look forward to. This hope strengthened his resolve to remain as faithful as he possibly could in the present, depending firmly on the help of the Holy Spirit.

'Prick him anywhere; and you will find that his blood is bibline [that is, biblical]'

Another Scripture in John's Gospel also helped him, this time John 16:33. Here Bunyan read that believers would have 'trouble' in this life. Nevertheless, they were to 'take heart', for Jesus had 'overcome' the world. The verse also spoke of deep peace. Here were promises both for the future and for the present, promises he could trust in because they had been spoken by his Lord, who had never let him down. He also came to trust God for his family. As far as this was concerned, an important text was Jeremiah 49:11. Here God said he would take care of widows and orphans. This was another wonderful promise to which the prisoner could cling. We can imagine him kneeling in his prison cell, wrestling in prayer as he worked his way towards a childlike trust in God in these difficult circumstances. Bunyan resolved to take God at His word.

In fact, as he speaks of his imprisonment, and how he endured, he mentions scripture after scripture. Further examples of verses and passages which helped him include 1 Peter 1:2, 1 Peter 2:16 and Colossians 3:3–4. C.H. Spurgeon once said of Bunyan, 'Prick him anywhere; and you will find that his blood is bibline [that is, biblical].' This truth can be seen particularly well as the prisoner responds to his time in jail. His heart and mind were soaked in the Bible and God spoke to him and encouraged him repeatedly as he meditated on it. It was as if the Scriptures themselves were flowing through his veins. They were his spiritual lifeblood.

I WILL PRAY WITH THE SPIRIT

Alongside reading and reflecting on the Bible, a second way Bunyan found help was in prayer. He quotes Colossians 1:11, in which Paul prays believers might be strengthened by the power of God, as one of the verses which encouraged him to persevere in prayer. Paul's petition was for 'patience', 'long suffering' and 'joyfulness' (AV), and Bunyan sought to intercede along the same lines. One of the works he published in the early years of his imprisonment was entitled *I Will Pray with the Spirit*. This sets out his overall approach to prayer.

I Will Pray with the Spirit was first published in 1662, two years into his prison sentence. A second edition quickly followed a year later, a sign Bunyan was becoming known as a writer and that his books were selling. In this short work, he makes some simple but profound points about his subject. He defines prayer for his readers, describing it as a 'pouring out of the heart or soul to God'. This could only be done, he insisted, 'through Christ' and with the aid of the Holy Spirit. Really, prayer should be impossible, for how could sinful human beings approach a holy God? But through Jesus' sacrifice and with the help of the Holy Spirit, it was possible to approach God; indeed, there was an open invitation for Christians to do so. Jesus had opened the way into the presence of the Father. Consequently, at any time and in any place – even in prison – believers could 'pour out' their hearts to Him and know they were heard.

Bunyan strongly disliked the use of set prayers or liturgy. This was an attitude which went hand-in-hand with his determined opposition to the Anglican Prayer Book. Spoken prayer should be in a person's own words, although of course they might well quote Scripture and use much biblical language as a prayer unfolded. He believed that liturgy encouraged empty, formal praying. The danger was that someone would read lines by rote without ever really engaging with them – or with God. What was important was that all prayer – whether it be praise, thanksgiving, confession or petition – came from the 'heart'. As he put it at one point in his book, 'Take heed that thy heart go to God as well as thy mouth.' For Bunyan, this was crucial.

He also gave advice as to the content of people's prayers. These, he insisted, should be shaped by the concerns and priorities of the Bible. Rather than just asking for what they wanted, he encouraged believers to search the Bible and allow the Scriptures rather than their own thoughts and feelings to shape their praise and petitions. He explained that when he was uncertain about what to pray for, he would ask the Holy Spirit to bring to mind Bible verses which could direct him. Bunyan's 'biblical blood' flowed through his prayer life, as it did through everything else.

In *I Will Pray with the Spirit*, Bunyan often wrote about his own experiences in prayer in ways he hoped would encourage his readers. There were times, he admitted, when he found it hard to maintain his focus when he was praying. However much he tried,

Right:
The jug Mary is reputed to have used to carry soup to her father

his mind kept wandering. On these occasions he would ask God to direct his wavering thoughts, effectively making his inability to focus in prayer the subject of his petition. He had found this a helpful practice, and so encouraged others to follow his example if they encountered similar difficulties. He also wrote of occasions when he went through 'fits of agony of spirit'. During these times of depression he openly and honestly confessed he was tempted to 'leave off' prayer altogether. His advice to people going through something similar was to 'cleave' ever closer to God and continue to cry to Him. At such times prayer might be without words, for true prayer might easily be in the form of 'sighs and groans'. What was important – indeed essential – was that it was from the heart.

So, he was not only sharing biblical thoughts on prayer with his readers, but his own journey in prayer, his struggles as well as his successes. Perhaps this is why the book became popular. Some writers talk about Bunyan as a giant in prayer. In many ways this is right, but he was more than willing to admit that he did not always find prayer easy, something we may well find an encouragement!

Through both prayer and the Bible, Bunyan found he was growing closer to Jesus. He is at pains to emphasise this in his writing about his prison experience. In *A Brief Account of the Author's Imprisonment* he says, 'Jesus Christ … was never more real or apparent than now; here I have seen Him and felt Him indeed.' He believed God Himself was standing with him in prison. As he read the Bible it often came alive to him and God and His ways were revealed with a freshness and an immediacy. 'I never had in all my life so great an inlet into the Word of God as now', he said. The context of suffering was important to his growing relationship with God. As Bunyan suffered for the sake of Christ, he found to his joy that Jesus, who had Himself suffered greatly, came near to him and strengthened him. His dark prison cell was transformed, becoming for him a place full of the light of God. The raw material of his prison experiences was being used to strengthen his faith.

MINISTRY

Another way Bunyan grew through being in prison was through engaging in ministry. As we've seen, on occasion this could take place outside the jail! But most of his service was conducted from behind bars. Other Nonconformists were being jailed for 'crimes' similar to Bunyan's, as we've already noted. A number of these men knew him, and he would sometimes preach to them and to any others who would listen in one of the jail's communal areas. The Christians tried to support each other through their prison experience, and Bunyan certainly played his part in this. Separated for the most part from the meetings of his Bedford church, he found God had given him a new congregation to share with.

However, the key way he began to minister was, of course, through his writing. By the early 1660s he was honing his skills and

beginning to show the ability that would set him apart as an author. In prison, as well as writing many of the works already mentioned, for example, *Grace Abounding* and *I Will Pray with the Spirit*, he composed a book of poetry, called *Profitable Meditations*, and wrote up several of his sermons for publication. One of the books, *The Holy City*, was based on a message that was actually preached within the confines of the prison. As Bunyan had stood up to give a word to his fellow inmates, he had felt 'empty, spiritless, and barren'. What's more, he had nothing prepared, either written down or in his head. How could he possibly speak to these people when both his heart and his head were empty? Leafing through his Bible he happened upon Revelation 21:11, with its description of the New Jerusalem coming down from heaven. He said a quick prayer for God's blessing (actually he speaks of uttering a few 'groans' to God – this was all he could manage) and launched into his subject.

As he began to preach, he realised God was speaking through him, and with particular power. As he warmed to his theme, he set forth the glory and wonder of the New Jerusalem. This was the future inheritance of all those who knew Jesus. As he did this, he urged his hearers to grasp this wonderful future hope and hold onto it by faith. Moreover, they were to let this glorious vision inform and shape the way they lived in the present day. By the time he had finished, both he and his hearers were thoroughly 'refreshed'. As Bunyan reflected on his preaching that day, he daringly compared his experience to that of Jesus who had blessed and then distributed the five loaves and two fish at the feeding of the 5,000 (Matt. 14:15–21). When Jesus broke the small amount of food and shared it, miraculously, there was more than enough for everyone. There were even twelve basketfuls left over. Similarly, said Bunyan, when he had broken the 'bread of life' which was the Word of God and shared it out, he had found there was enough for everyone, despite his meagre preparation. He pressed the image still further, saying that at the end of the message he still had a whole 'basketful' of bread left over. This was some of the material he used to help him write

Left:

Bunyan preaching in Bedford, 18 October 1659. The old town bridge and lock-up can be seen in the background

The Holy City, which is a greatly expanded version of the sermon.

How did Bunyan the prisoner manage to get these books published? This is a good question! It can't have been easy. Many people assume Elizabeth took the manuscripts to London and hawked them around different publishers known to be sympathetic to Nonconformists. Although no one knows for certain, this is probably what happened. Her task would become considerably easier as her husband's fame grew but publishing his work would still be a risky business. Many printers and booksellers were being prosecuted for either producing or selling works by Nonconformists. *I Will Pray with the Spirit*, with its sharp criticisms of the *Book of Common Prayer*, would have been considered especially suspect by the authorities. Most likely because of this, the surviving early editions of this particular work do not carry the name of any publisher. If the book was discovered in someone's possession, then it would be difficult to trace it back to the printer, who would therefore have a better chance of avoiding prosecution. Of course, one of the benefits of Bunyan's writing was that it provided a source of income for him and his family, one that was significantly more fruitful than making shoelaces. He did not make much money – he was hardly in a position to bargain for good rates. But he made enough. God was indeed looking after the 'widows and orphans' who were his family, making good on the promise of Jeremiah 49:11. And Bunyan himself was able to grow through his prison experience. It was never easy: in fact, at times it was incredibly tough. But through it he grew closer to God and became more and more useful in God's service. Just how useful will be seen in the next chapter, which deals with the work for which Bunyan is best known and which was also composed in prison – *The Pilgrim's Progress*.

GOING FURTHER

Many themes could be followed up in this section. The importance of engaging with God in prayer is an obvious one. On this subject, Bunyan has much to say that is valuable for Christians today. I especially like his close linking of prayer and Bible reading, with the content of Scripture shaping the content of our prayers. His blanket rejection of liturgy should be questioned. The Bible itself contains written prayers (not least the 150 psalms) which Christians have used down the ages as an aid to devotion. His dislike of the Church of England and its Prayer Book led him to overstate his case. But he was surely right in saying there is a danger that 'reading a prayer' can become a dry and formal exercise. We might add that this can happen with extempore prayer too! We repeat stock words and phrases without our hearts being truly engaged. Bunyan reminds us true prayer is nothing less than deep heart, mind and soul engagement with God. As he says, 'When you pray, rather let your heart be without words than your words without heart.' And his example is certainly as good as his teaching. He didn't just write about prayer: he was himself a real man of prayer, engaging heart-to-heart with God. All of this is of vital importance for anyone who wants to 'go further' on their Christian journey.

Yet what especially strikes me about the material in this chapter is the way Bunyan grew as a Christian disciple through suffering. His difficulties drove him closer to God, forcing him to rely on his Lord all the more. God revealed more about His character and His ways to Bunyan as he suffered. As far as his ministry was concerned, his experiences in prison further increased his empathy with those who faced similar difficulties, or perhaps different struggles which were just as real. This, and his growing closeness to God, made him increasingly effective in sharing with others. Writing was going to be the key way God used him and, at a very basic level, as a prisoner he now had more time to do this. If he had not been incarcerated, he would have been increasingly in demand both as preacher and pastor. Almost certainly, Bunyan would have replaced John Burton as pastor of the Bedford church in 1660 if he had not been imprisoned. Would he have had the time to develop his writing skills and to produce so many books and pamphlets if he had been working full tilt as a pastor and travelling preacher? The answer is surely, 'no'. Yet again, Romans 8:28 is relevant. God was bringing good out of a seemingly desperate situation. The fact Bunyan thrived in prison had a lot to do with his willingness to learn and grow through suffering.

YOUR OWN JOURNEY

I have already emphasised at the close of previous chapters how Bunyan's life shows God's sustaining power in difficult times. The material in this present chapter suggests something more. God wants to work in our difficult circumstances to bring about personal growth and to make us more effective in ministry. This can be a hard truth to accept but it is a biblical one. As well as Romans 8:28, the opening verses of 1 Peter, especially 1:5–6, are highly relevant. In these Peter speaks of the 'grief' the Christians to whom he is writing have suffered in 'all kinds of trials'. Even so, the believers are to 'rejoice'. How can this be? The answer is in verse 6. Trials can 'refine' a Christian's faith. The image of refining is a powerful one. Just as precious metal is purified by being subject to tremendous heat, with the dross being burnt off, so our precious faith is refined by going through the 'fire' of different trials. It is a potent image, one Bunyan the metal worker might well have appreciated, although he was never rich enough to work with any precious materials!

Of course, intense suffering is terribly difficult to take. Those who experience grief, pain, confusion and darkness can fall back in the Christian life and even turn from God completely. I understand why this happens, and I believe God still loves those who respond in this way, and wants to draw them back to Him. But if we cooperate with God in what He wants to do in our lives, the result of our suffering is that our faith will be refined, just as Bunyan's was. This refining then leads to Christian growth and increased fruitfulness in ministry. As people say, suffering can make us 'bitter' or it can make us 'better'. Bunyan chose the latter option. How do we respond as we go through suffering?

Joshua Symonds

Samuel Hillyard

Samuel Sanderson

John Jukes

John Brown

W. Charter Piggott

Ebenezer Chandler

William J. Coates

• CHAPTER 7 •

John Bunyan

Leonard Brooks

Samuel Fenn

C. Bernard Cockett

THE PILGRIM'S PROGRESS

John Whiteman

Ralph H. Turner

John Burton

Leonard J. Towers

John Gifford

James W. Alexander

✠ TO THE GLORY OF GOD AND IN COMMEMORATION OF ✠
THE TER-CENTENARY OF BUNYAN MEETING (1650-1950)
Evangelist (John Gifford, Minister 1650-55) points the way to Christian (John Bunyan, Minister 1671-88)

FROM WRITING TO PUBLICATION

**B**unyan almost certainly began to write the book which would make him famous in the late 1660s when he was still in Bedford County Jail. No one knows for sure when he completed it, but it was not published until 1678, perhaps ten years after he picked up his pen in his prison cell to jot down his first thoughts. For Bunyan, who tended to work at a fast pace, this delay was unusual. Most likely he was concerned with how people might react to this particular book. He knew his enemies wouldn't like it of course. They would be angry to see yet another work from that troublemaker, John Bunyan. But might there also be faithful Christians – those who had appreciated his earlier books – who would think his use of allegory inappropriate? For this new production was not spiritual autobiography, like *Grace Abounding*, or a straightforward treatise on prayer, like *I Will Pray with the Spirit*. The story he entitled *The Pilgrim's Progress* was exactly that – a story, one full of imagined places and characters, with plenty of fast-paced action and vivid dialogue. To be sure it was a story based on the realities of the Christian life, one which conveyed vital spiritual truths to the reader. But this in itself could have spelt danger for the author. Was it right to take something as serious as the Christian 'pilgrimage' and dramatise it in this way? There had been nothing quite like it in English literature before. In the seventeenth-century world this approach was new and daring, not to say very risky.

Some of Bunyan's friends advised him not to publish. He would only be stirring up more trouble for himself. Fortunately, he eventually went ahead and courageously submitted the book to Nathaniel Ponder, a London publisher. Ponder was an enthusiastic Nonconformist who had already been imprisoned for printing an unlicensed pamphlet. He was willing to take a chance with

Left:

Doors at the

Bedford Meeting

depicting

scenes from

The Pilgrim's

Progress

Bunyan's exciting new work. In 1678 the slim book with just over 200 printed pages appeared, priced at one shilling and sixpence.

Bunyan's friends had been right about one thing: the book caused a great stir, so much so that by 1680 an expanded fourth edition was being rushed through the printers. In a publisher's note attached to this edition, Nathaniel Ponder wrote *The Pilgrim's Progress* had met with a 'good acceptation among the people'. This was a considerable understatement. Thanks to the popularity of the book, Bunyan was becoming well known far beyond his Bedford base. And this was only the beginning. By 1692, just four years after the author's death, an estimated 100,000 copies were in print in England, with the book already translated into languages as varied as French, Dutch and Welsh. In another era, both Bunyan and Ponder would have made a fortune. But copyright laws were not what they are today and unscrupulous publishers started to produce their own editions, printing thousands of volumes without permission and selling them cheaply. Ponder tried to take his rivals – 'land pirates' he called them – to court. But he failed to get justice, and the 'pirated' editions continued to appear unchecked. To make matters worse he had spent such large sums on legal fees that he ended up ruining himself and his business. In 1688 Ponder was in prison again – this time because of crippling debt. Although he was released, his final years continued to be dogged by ongoing financial difficulty. The publisher of one of the greatest works of literature the world has ever seen died in poverty in June 1699.

... Bunyan himself gained little financially from his extraordinary success

This helps to explain why Bunyan himself gained little financially from his extraordinary success. The vast amounts of money made from his work went into the undeserving pockets of others. But he came to believe he had become rich in another far more significant way. He had grown in knowledge and love of God through his writing and had helped countless others to make progress in their own Christian faith. For Bunyan, this was great reward.

GETTING TO GRIPS WITH *THE PILGRIM'S PROGRESS*

Different editions of *The Pilgrim's Progress* are, of course, widely available today, as are summaries of the plot and attempts to retell the story in a way that will help modern readers engage with it more easily. I don't want to duplicate what is available elsewhere, but I do want to encourage you to get to grips with Bunyan's masterpiece, and set out at least some of the deep spiritual lessons present on every page of the book. In this chapter we focus on six key 'scenes'. Much will have to be left out, but approaching *The Pilgrim's Progress* in this way helps us think about some of its lessons in more depth, whilst still enabling us to get to grips with the basic shape of the story. Hopefully, it will also act as an encouragement for you to read this wonderful narrative for yourself.

Scene 1: Through the wicket gate

The first 'scene' we are going to look at is the conversion of Bunyan's pilgrim, called 'Christian' (although, as he later says in the story, the name 'Graceless' would have been more appropriate at this beginning stage). Christian leaves the 'City of Destruction', having failed in his attempts to persuade his wife and children to follow him. In a section full of pathos, as he finally sets off they 'cry after him to return'. Full of misery, he has to put his fingers in his ears to block out the heartrending sound. The deep sadness remains with him. Later in the story he weeps at the thought they are not accompanying him on this journey of all journeys.

As he walks away from the City of Destruction, he has a huge 'burden' on his back, symbolising the heavy load of sin he carries. Early on, he meets various characters who try to persuade him to return to the City and, bogged down, he spends time in the 'Slough of Despond'. But a character named Evangelist has, with loving and 'trembling' concern, directed Christian to a 'little Wicket Gate' (meaning a small gate or door, often built into a larger one). Eventually, the weary traveller arrives. Over the gate he sees the words, 'Knock, and it shall be opened unto you' from Matthew 7:7 (AV).

Christian reads the text and duly bangs on the door.

On the other side of the gate is a man called 'Good-Will' who asks Christian why he has come. The would-be pilgrim explains about his flight from the City of Destruction and the words of Evangelist (who, as already noted in Chapter Two, was probably modelled on Bunyan's pastor and friend, John Gifford). Christian knows he is undeserving and a 'poor burdened sinner', and half believes he will be refused entrance. But, to his joy, Good-Will lives up to his name, for he is 'willing with all his heart' to let him through. The gate is unfastened and the way is open. The pilgrim is pulled through the gate, a wonderful picture of the gracious action of God who draws us to Himself. This is the moment of conversion in the story, and now the name 'Christian' is fully appropriate.

Bunyan wants to emphasise, in the light of his own experiences and struggles for assurance, that Jesus will receive all who truly turn to Him. A marginal note in most editions reassures the anxious reader 'The gate will be opened to broken-hearted sinners' and, in the story itself, Good-Will makes it clear there is free and full forgiveness for all sinners who come in faith. Bunyan's beautiful, sensitive picture of Christian conversion has helped many weary men and women out of their own 'Slough of Despond', enabling them to find forgiveness and take their own first steps in the Christian life.

But this, of course, is only the beginning. Now Good-Will says to Christian, 'Good Christian, come a little way with me ... Look before thee; doest thou see this narrow way? That is the way thou must go.' He goes on to explain this way is a 'straight' and 'narrow' way. There is a danger he might get lost, for there are other paths which are 'crooked' and 'wide' that branch off from the true way. These might seem attractive alternatives, but they will lead to disaster. Christian is urged to stick to the narrow way whatever temptations there might be to stray onto a different route.

Interestingly, at this stage Christian still has the heavy, crushing burden on his back. We might expect it to fall off right here.

Right:
Christian
loses his
burden at
the cross

Christian tries to remove it, but he is unable to take it off. Good-Will tells him, 'As to the burden, be content to bear it, until thou comest to the place of deliverance; for there it will fall off thy back itself.' Another marginal notes says, 'There is no deliverance from the guilt and burden of sin but by the death and blood of Christ.' Bunyan wants to emphasise the importance of the cross as the place where we are truly set free from sin and guilt. The scene where this happens is one of the most important in the book.

Scene 2: Christian loses his burden at the cross

Soon after Christian passes through the Wicket Gate, he spends time at the 'Interpreter's House'. Here the 'Interpreter' explains more about the way of discipleship. As Christian is about to leave, Interpreter gives him a 'blessing'. 'The Comforter be always with thee good Christian, to guide thee in the way that leads to the [Celestial] City.' The pilgrim's journey ahead would be difficult, but he has now received instruction from the Bible and has the assurance the 'Comforter' – that is, the Holy Spirit – will be with him.

He Hath Given Me Rest By His Sorrow And Life By His Death

As Christian continues on his way he starts running, but not without 'great difficulty', because of the great load he is carrying. But, after a while, 'burdened Christian' comes to a hill upon which there is a cross and, a little below it on the hillside, an open, empty 'sepulchre' or tomb. Wonderfully, as Christian approached the cross,

His burden loosed from off his shoulders, and fell from off his back; and began to tumble, and so continued to do till it came to the mouth of the sepulchre, where it fell in, and I saw it no more. Then was Christian glad

and lightsome, and said with a merry heart, 'He hath given me rest by his sorrow, and life by his death.' Then he stood still a while, to look and to wonder; for it was very surprising to him that the sight of the Cross should thus ease him of his burden. He looked therefore, and looked again, even till the springs that were in his head sent the waters down his cheeks.

This beautiful piece of writing is a great example of Bunyan's style and way with words. To be sure, some of his language can seem a little strange to us today. But it is still extremely powerful. For me, the description of Christian as 'lightsome' evokes his joy quite brilliantly, especially as it contrasts so well with the severe, heavy burden which has just rolled away. The final sentence, with the 'springs' in Christian's head sending 'waters down his cheeks' is a striking, poetic description of the tears that fell as he contemplated the cross and what this meant for him. This deep

emotional response is appropriate for all those who have been set free from sin and guilt, and who realise the immense cost Christ paid to make this possible.

Christian then gives 'three leaps for joy' and starts to sing, 'Blessed Cross! Blessed Sepulchre! Blessed … be the man that there was put to shame for me!' This is one of the passages from Bunyan's writing which gives the lie to Puritans being grim, dour and lacking emotion. Christian is full of joy as he goes on his way, and this bursts out of him in lively dancing and singing. Here is happiness which just has to be expressed. Such delight was also felt by the author himself as he thought about the cross, and all that his Saviour Jesus had accomplished for him there. But Bunyan the prisoner also knew that the Christian life, joyful as it was, was demanding and difficult. As Christian journeyed on, there would be many problems, some of which threatened to overwhelm him. Nevertheless, the cross was a huge turning point.

Scene 3: The 'Hill Difficulty' and the roaring lions

Before long, Christian comes to a place where the way seems to split in three. It is at the foot of a steep, forbidding-looking hill. The path which comes from the Wicket Gate heads straight up the hill. But there are two other paths, one branching off to the right, the other to the left. At this point in his journey, Christian is travelling with two companions, 'Formalist' and 'Hypocrisy'. The straight way looks too difficult for them, and they each take one of the easier paths. Neither is seen again. Christian pauses to drink from a spring in order to refresh himself (another sure reference to the Holy Spirit) and then determinedly sets off up the hill, which is called 'Difficulty'. To begin with he runs, but the way is too steep and rough and he ends up clambering on his hands and knees. Eventually he approaches the 'Palace Beautiful'. Surely he will find shelter and rest here! But there are two lions barring the way! In fact, they are chained so that they cannot quite reach the path, although they can come very close. But Christian does

Left:

Christian climbs

the Hill Difficulty

not see the chains. He believes the lions are loose and is terrified. He stops, thinking that to go forward is certain death. Perhaps he should even turn back. In Bunyan's racy narrative, full of action and gripping adventure, here is another pivotal moment.

The porter of the Palace Beautiful, whose name is 'Watchful', sees what is happening and cries out to encourage the faltering pilgrim,

> *Is thy strength so small? Fear not the lions, for they are chained and are placed there for trial of faith where it is; and for discovery of those that have none: keep in the midst of the path, and no hurt shall come unto thee.*

Christian was hesitant. Indeed he was still 'trembling with fear' because of the ferocious beasts. But now he starts to move forward again,

> *He went on … taking good heed to the directions of the porter; he heard [the lions] roar, but they did him no harm. Then he clapped his hands, and went on till he came and stood at the gate where the porter was.*

The pilgrim had made it – just. He (and the reader) breathe a sigh of relief. The tired Christian rests at the Palace Beautiful, which he learns has been built by the 'Lord of the Hill' for the 'relief and security of pilgrims', so they can be refreshed before continuing on their way. Through his story, Bunyan encourages all Christians to stick to God's path – the straight and narrow way (see Matt. 7:13–14). Often this is a difficult way, but it is still the right way. As we follow this route we know God's protection. It is when we wander off the path that we leave ourselves open to attack. Also, in this part of the story, the author reminds us of the lesson we saw he learned in prison: trials and temptations test and strengthen our faith (1 Pet. 1:6–7). When we come through such trials, our faith is proved to be genuine. So, the dramatic story teaches us vital lessons in the life of discipleship. But for Bunyan's pilgrim, even greater trials were ahead.

Right:
Scenes from
the Saltmine
Theatre Company
production of
*The Pilgrim's
Progress*

Scene 4: Vanity Fair

As Christian continues on he meets all sorts of dangerous challenges, but he also meets a fellow pilgrim, 'Faithful'. Many of those he has met so far on his journey have been unhelpful, such as Formalist and Hypocrisy (others I've not mentioned include 'Pliable' and 'Worldly-Wiseman'). But 'Faithful' is different. He helps Christian when he has stumbled and fallen on the path. Christian calls him 'my honoured and well-beloved brother'. Their relationship is movingly described and stands as an example of the close, spiritual friendship which can exist between fellow believers. They are able to share experiences and encourage each other as they walk together. We are not called to live the Christian life alone, for God gives us friends like Faithful who can help us along the way. But in Bunyan's story, the bond between Christian and Faithful is about to be tested to the limit.

The two pilgrims approach a town called 'Vanity', within which is a Fair, 'Vanity-Fair'. The two men have not turned from the straight and narrow way. Rather, Vanity-Fair has been set up by the devil so the true path goes right through it, so he can deliberately cause problems for the pilgrims. Bunyan depicts the Fair as a place in which every kind of wickedness flourishes. There is vice and immorality; indeed, prostitution and adultery are rife. There is much law-breaking, including theft and what is called crime 'of a blood red colour', that is, murder. Interestingly, there is also injustice and inequality, with 'honours, preferments', and 'titles' bought and sold to the highest bidder, just as they were in the England of the Restoration. Finally, there is rank materialism. All sorts of merchandise is sold, 'bodies, souls, silver, gold, pearls, precious stones, and what not'. The list is instructive. People – bodies and souls – have been reduced to the level of commodities in Vanity-Fair. They are not so much human beings as goods which can be traded along with everything else. Here is a materialistic, consumerist society in which everything, and every person, has a price. And the price of life is very cheap, as Christian and Faithful are about to discover.

Right:
Martyrdom at
Vanity-Fair

The pilgrims enter the Fair and they are immediately in trouble. They are marked out by their different way of speaking and by their refusal to buy the wares for sale. Christian and Faithful are despised by the traders and by the restless, noisy, milling crowds, with 'some mocking, some taunting, some speaking reproachfully, and some calling upon others to smite them'. Soon all order – such as it was – has broken down in the place, so that 'the Fair was almost overturned'. Christian and Faithful are arrested and locked in a cage, where they are abused by the local populace. This is mob rule, and the plight of the pilgrims is about to get worse.

Bunyan's harrowing description of what happens next draws from the treatment meted out to Jesus and His apostles, and also from more recent martyrdoms (*Foxe's Book of Martyrs*, we remember, was at his side in prison). He is also influenced by his knowledge of what was happening around the country in his own day and, of course, his own sad experience of arrest, trial and imprisonment. In *The Pilgrim's Progress*, Faithful and Christian are beaten, clapped in 'irons' and led in their chains through the town. This is partly to humiliate them, but it is also to terrorise any who might speak on their behalf at the forthcoming trial, for there are at least some in the town who have been attracted by the different way of life the two men embody. The pilgrims bear their cruel treatment with a 'meekness and patience' which echoes the attitude of Jesus when He was accused, but Christian and Faithful's gentle behaviour only sends the accusers into an even 'greater rage'. The two men know full well what might be about to happen, but they commit themselves into the care of a sovereign and loving God. One of them is indeed about to pay the ultimate price for his faith.

For Bunyan to write in this way ... when he was at the mercy of the authorities was brave indeed ...

Bunyan makes it clear that the 'trial' is completely rigged: 'They brought them forth to their trial in order to their condemnation', he says. The character of the judge, 'Lord Hategood' was probably based, at least in part, on the judges and magistrates like Sir John Kelynge whom Bunyan knew through his own appearances before the courts. Faithful insists he is a 'man of peace', but the unjust judge is having none of it. The witnesses hurl accusations at the defendants. Men like 'Envy' and 'Superstition' make their bogus accusations. The jury is made up of characters such as 'Mr Liar', 'Mr No-Good', 'Mr Cruelty' and 'Mr Hate-Light'. The foreman of the jury is 'Mr Blind-Man', who ironically says, 'I see clearly that this man [Faithful] is an heretic'! The proceedings are a mockery of justice from start to finish. Many of Bunyan's readers would have recognised the connections between the trial at Vanity-Fair and the treatment of conscientious, principled Nonconformists in their own day. For Bunyan to write in this way in prison when he was at the mercy of the authorities was brave indeed, for at any point his manuscript might have been discovered.

Because Faithful has spoken at the trial it is he who is condemned to death, a death that is as cruel as the trial has been crooked. He is beaten, stabbed, stoned and then finally, in treatment which echoes that given to the sixteenth-century martyrs, burned to death. Bunyan does not go into great detail about this; the horror of Faithful's death is described quickly. It is horrific, nevertheless. Yet for the martyr, this unjust, agonising death is the gateway to the Celestial City. Bunyan puts it like this,

> *Now, I saw that there stood before the multitude a chariot and a couple of horses waiting for Faithful, who (so soon as his adversaries had despatched him) was taken up into it, and straightway was carried up through the clouds, with sound of trumpet, the nearest way to the Celestial Gate.*

For Faithful, all pain had gone. We might expect Christian to follow in the same way, but, inexplicably, he is merely remanded in prison. Perhaps the blood-lust of the authorities and the crowd had been satisfied – for now. He remains in jail for a while but, mysteriously, he 'escapes' his captors. We are not told how. Was he simply released? Did he escape – perhaps in circumstances similar to John Gifford's escape from his Parliamentary captors after the Battle of Maidstone? What we do know is that Bunyan attributes this miraculous deliverance to 'He that over-rules all things'. God is in control. Our times are in His hands.

Scene 5: Wandering from the path

The witness of Faithful and Christian at Vanity-Fair has borne some fruit, for at least one person within the town has been deeply struck by the behaviour of these pilgrims under fire. Their example and testimony have given him hope of a different life, a better life, and so this inhabitant of Vanity-Fair joins Christian on his journey. Because he is now a man of hope, 'Hopeful' becomes his name. There are still many perils ahead. They pass through the town of 'Fair-speech', full of smooth-talking but faithless people such as the super-rich,

silver-tongued Lord Turn-about and the shifty Lord Time-server, men who totally lack the rugged principles and commitment to God Faithful had shown. For Bunyan, such a place is just as dangerous as Vanity-Fair. The temptations to step back from complete Christian commitment are different, more subtle than the full-frontal onslaught which the pilgrims faced in Vanity-Fair, but just as real. The two pilgrims are grateful to leave the town and continue on their way.

Their worst trouble comes when they leave the narrow path for a seemingly better route – in fact, it is Christian who leads Hopeful astray. The new path was, to begin with, 'very easy for their feet' and seems to run parallel to the narrow way, which is the reason Christian was deceived. But when night draws in they realise their foolishness. In the darkness the rain begins to fall, followed by heavy thunder and lightning which crashes down 'in a very dreadful manner'. Then the water around them begins to rise. In fact, it comes up so quickly there is imminent danger of drowning. Has Christian come so far only to be lost after all? What's more, has he led his friend astray as well?

In a desperate state, they find some shelter. But the place they discover is called 'Doubting-Castle', inhabited by the ominously named 'Giant-Despair'. Here they are plunged into a state of dejection, repeatedly beaten down by the cruel Giant. Christian is especially low. Hopeful turns out to be a wonderful friend, repeatedly encouraging and strengthening his companion. It is hard to read this section of *The Pilgrim's Progress* without thinking of Bunyan's own protracted doubts and struggles, as chronicled at length in *Grace Abounding*. If he had been able to turn to such a friend, perhaps he would have found his way out of his own 'Doubting-Castle' sooner than he did. Eventually, Christian discovers he has a key called 'Promise' which unlocks the castle doors and enables their escape. Bunyan's point is clear enough. The promises of God are the keys which enable us to escape doubt and despair. The doubts may be great, but God's promises are greater still, so that even the heaviest door will swing open when the key is used.

The two men have yet more dangerous encounters, including one with 'Atheist' who scoffs at them and calls them 'ignorant'. But

Left:

Scenes from the Saltmine Theatre Company production of *The Pilgrim's Progress* still they press on, refusing to be deterred. At last they approach their destination. The Celestial City! But the City is made of 'pure gold' and is so 'glorious' that the pilgrims 'could not, as yet, with open face behold it'. They are very near the goal of their journey, but still they are having to walk by faith (2 Cor. 5:7). And there is one more test yet to come.

The final scene: The 'River of Death' and the 'Celestial City'

By now other pilgrims have joined Christian and Hopeful, and they arrive at last within clear site of the City Gate. But between them and this Gate is a river, and there is no bridge. To get into the Celestial City they will somehow have to cross the river: there is no other way. Not for the first time Christian hesitates, but at last he steps fearfully out into the water. Almost immediately, he begins to sink.

Christian cries out to Hopeful, in words which echo those found in the Psalms, 'I sink in deep water, the billows go over my head, all His waves go over me' (eg Psa. 42:7, AV). Hopeful responds, 'Be of good cheer, my brother, I feel the bottom, and it is good.' Yet Christian is not to be comforted. A 'great darkness and horror' falls upon him. His mind is full of the sins he had committed – both before and after he embarked on his pilgrimage. Perhaps he is not forgiven after all! To make matters worse, he is severely tried with 'apparitions of hobgoblins and evil spirits'. Hopeful struggles to keep his friend's head above water. Christian sinks and then rises, sinks and then rises again. Hopeful (who comes into his own in this story) encourages his fellow pilgrim further: 'Be of good cheer, Jesus Christ maketh thee whole,' he urges. This is the turning point in the crossing, for,

> *With that, Christian brake out with a loud voice, 'Oh I see Him again! And He tells me, 'When thou passest through the waters, I will be with thee, and through the rivers, they shall not overflow thee' [Isa. 43:2, AV]. Then they both took courage, and the enemy was after that as still as stone, until they were gone over.*

Death – symbolised by the river – had been an ordeal indeed, more for Christian than for Hopeful, but difficult still for them both. Yet by focusing on Jesus and trusting in Him they had come through.

The two pilgrims are met by two 'Shining Ones', angelic beings who conduct them into the Celestial City. Bunyan's depiction of this is packed full of biblical language and imagery. As they approach the City, the Shining Ones describe it in the following words,

> *'There', they say, 'is the Mount Sion, the heavenly Jerusalem, the innumerable company of angels, and the spirits of just men made perfect; you are going now,' said they, 'to the Paradise of God, wherein you shall see the Tree of Life, and eat of the never-fading fruits thereof; and when you come there you shall have white robes given you, and your walk and talk shall every day be with the King, even all the days of eternity. There you shall not see again such things as you saw when you were in the lower region upon the earth … sorrow, sickness, affliction, and death, 'for the former things are passed away'.*

Thus, the future for Christian, Hopeful, and the other pilgrims who enter the Celestial City with them is glorious and eternal. And not just for them. For this is the sure and certain future for all those in any age who trust in Christ and follow Him along the 'straight and narrow way'.

◤ GOING FURTHER

I hope I have, in some small way, encouraged you to read Bunyan for yourself. If so, *The Pilgrim's Progress* is *the* place to start, with its excitement, drama, cliffhanging scenes and emotional highs and lows. Because the work was written so long ago, people can sometimes find parts of it difficult, especially its longer sections of dialogue. This is quite understandable. But for those who persevere – rather like Bunyan's pilgrim who kept on with his journey whether the going was easy or difficult – there are great rewards to be had.

It's important to read new Christian books. I want to encourage this (obviously!), not least because we need to relate our faith to the times and culture we live in today. But it's important to read older Christian books too, especially the real classics which have stood the test of time. Listen to what C.S. Lewis has to say,

> Since I myself am a writer, I do not wish the ordinary reader to read no modern books. But if he must read only the new or only the old, I would advise him to read the old ... A new book is still on its trial and (we are) not in a position to judge it. It has to be tested against the great body of Christian thought down the ages, and all its hidden implications, often unsuspected by the author himself, have to be brought to light.[11]

The Christian classics *have* stood the test of time. They challenge our modern ways of thinking and enable us to see central truths in surprising and fresh ways. Reading these older books helps deliver us from just following the latest fads and fancies and roots us in the historic Christian faith. Unsurprisingly, Lewis lists Bunyan under the list of authors he believes are really important. What I want to encourage is a slow, careful, reflective reading of a book like *The Pilgrim's Progress*. You may not find it easy (although some fall in love with his writing straightaway) but stick with it, for the benefits will be immense. Bunyan's greatest work has much to say to us today.

 YOUR OWN JOURNEY

Even if we do not read *The Pilgrim's Progress* from cover to cover, the different 'scenes' we have looked at in this chapter each have a huge amount to teach us. Bunyan does not want us to read his story in a cool and detached way. He wants to draw us in so that we really engage with what he is writing on a personal level, for the realities of which the allegory speaks are more important than life and death itself.

A way of applying this to our own lives might be to ask ourselves the following question, 'Where do I place myself in this story?' It might be that as you reflect on the first scene, you recognise you

Right:
Selection of
editions of
*The Pilgrim's
Progress*

have not yet gone through the 'Wicket Gate', that is, that you have still not experienced Christian conversion. If so, you can be assured, as 'Christian' was, that God is willing to open the door to all who knock (Matt. 7:7). Perhaps you are a Christian, but need assurance that your 'burden' of sin has been dealt with at the cross, indeed that your sin and guilt have been taken away (Isa. 6:7; Heb. 10:22). If so, you can be certain that there is complete forgiveness thanks to the death of Christ. You might even want to picture the great weight of sin and guilt falling from your back and rolling away before being

swallowed up to be seen no more. Because of Christ's dying and rising this is what has actually happened with all who trust in Him. May you know the wonderful joy and freedom of Bunyan's pilgrim as you grasp this foundational gospel truth for yourself.

Alternatively, you may be really struggling. This may be your fault – you have wandered from the Christian path – or it may just be the circumstances you find yourself in. But whether you are toiling up 'Hill Difficulty', struggling to witness for God in 'Vanity-Fair', or locked up in 'Doubting-Castle' you can know God is more than able to bring you through. This is true even if you have wandered from the narrow way, for God wants to bring you back, however far you have strayed. Finally, you may be facing your final battle, death, or you may be living with a great fear of crossing this 'river'. I find Bunyan's treatment of this so helpful, because it takes seriously the Bible's understanding of death as the 'last enemy' (1 Cor. 15:26). Death is still real and it is still an 'enemy' we have to reckon with. It is normal for believers to have some fear as they approach it. Christian's anxieties – we might say panic – as he crosses the River of Death remind us of this. And yet, although the crossing can be difficult, God brings us through. And what is waiting for us on the other side of the river is truly wonderful. Bunyan describes it well, but the reality will be so much greater! God's promises sustained Christian to the end. Those same promises assure us the best is yet to be.

CHAPTER 8

BUNYAN THE PASTOR

Samuel Sanderson

Joshua Symonds

Samuel Hillyard

John Jukes

John Brown

W. Charter Piggott

Ebenezer Chandler

William J. Coates

John Bunyan

Leonard Brooks

Samuel Fenn

C. Bernard Cockett

John Whiteman

Ralph H. Turner

John Burton

Leonard T. Towers

John Gifford

James W. Alexander

TO THE GLORY OF GOD AND IN COMMEMORATION OF
THE TER-CENTENARY OF BUNYAN MEETING (1650-1950)
Evangelist (John Gifford, Minister 1650-55) points the way to Christian (John Bunyan, Minister 1671-88)

A BOOKE

Containing a Record of the Acts of

A

Congregation, of Christ, in, and about

BEDFORD.

And

A Briefe Account of their first

GATHERING

Matt, 28. 20. So I am with you always, even unto
the end of the world, amen.

Rev. 2. 10. Be thou faithful unto death, & I will give
thee a crown of life.

By whom alone the precious spark of liberty has been kindled & preserved
and to whom the English owe the whole freedom of their constitution
they appeared against the prerogative and receive the fire of
all the enemies of the constitution and prot't religion with
unshaken firmness

**B**unyan's imprisonment dragged on. Yes, he was able to use the time wisely and grow through it and, yes, his confinement gave him the time to write the extraordinary journey of the imagination that is *The Pilgrim's Progress*. But these positives should not blind us to the personal pain of his continued incarceration. Would Bunyan ever be released, or would he end up spending the rest of his days languishing in jail?

Encouragingly, by September 1669 things seemed to be looking up. As had been the case earlier in his imprisonment, he was occasionally allowed out and so was able to visit his church and family. The Bedford church book records he attended a number of their meetings, and they even asked him to visit some of the members in their homes. These moderate freedoms lasted into the new year. This was good for Bunyan and good for the church. What's more, might this new, relaxed prison regime mean he was about to be released? It seemed a genuine possibility.

But in May 1670 these hopes were cruelly dashed. This month saw a renewed wave of persecution directed against Dissenters. Bunyan found himself closely confined once again, and his church started experiencing increased persecution too. On Sunday 15 May the authorities raided the Bedford congregation while they were meeting for worship. Twenty-eight people were arrested. The preacher, one Nehemiah Coxe, was imprisoned along with Bunyan. Other congregation members were hit with fines and some had their property confiscated. On 22 May, a week after the initial raid, they bravely came together again, despite the threat of more, even heavier fines. Once more the service was raided and broken up by force. This book is the story of the famous John Bunyan, who through his writings became known throughout the world. But it is also the story of men and women we have never

Left:

The Bedford 'church book'

heard of who bravely refused to bow to persecution. The Bedford church book and other contemporary sources give us some of their names and trades. They include John Fenne, a hat-maker (who, like Nehemiah Coxe, spent time in prison with Bunyan); Mary Tilney, a 'gentlewoman' (who was given an especially large fine because she was relatively well off); Thomas Honylove, a cobbler (that is, a shoe-maker); and Thomas Arthur, a pipe-maker. These faithful people deserve to have their names recorded and honoured here. Together with others of the Bedford congregation, they provide us with a wonderful example of courage and commitment under fire.

RELEASE

Fortunately, in 1671, the tide of persecution began to recede. Bunyan started to enjoy some freedoms again and now there seemed a real prospect that his long imprisonment might be about to end. The Bedford church sensed this too. For a long time they had recognised Bunyan's gift and calling, not just as a writer (which for them was secondary) but as a preacher and encourager. In November he was appointed an elder of the church. Then – on 21 December 1671 – they called him as their pastor. This was an appointment they were prepared to make even though at this time he was still a prisoner. The church book puts it like this:

> *After much seeking God by prayer and sober conference ... the Congregation did at this meeting with joint consent (signified by solemn lifting up of their hands) call forth and appoint our brother John Bunyan to the pastoral office.*

The immediate future seemed bright. Bunyan was present at the meeting which called him, a further indication of the increasingly lax attitude of his captors. It seemed he would have the opportunity to exercise a ministry for which he was eminently suited, one that would give him much joy.

Right:
Bunyan's
communion
table

Nevertheless, at the end of February 1672, he was still having to spend most of his time in jail. Was this to be another 'false dawn' for Bunyan? Would he have to remain in prison despite expectations of his release being so high? This would have been a terrible blow indeed, but fortunately his long period behind bars was finally coming to an end. The breakthrough came in March when Charles II issued his so-called 'Declaration of Indulgence'. This allowed for the release of Nonconformists who were prisoners of conscience, and also gave leave for Dissenting churches to meet together. There were limits to the new freedoms and there was a danger they could be snatched back at any moment. The Parliament was now staunchly Royalist and there were many who thought the king had been overly generous. For them, the more Bunyan and his friends were persecuted the better. But still, this fragile situation was a great improvement on what had gone before. Bunyan was not formally pardoned until 13 September 1672, but all the evidence suggests he was free before this date. Probably he was released sometime in April. After twelve long years, he was able to walk the streets of Bedford without having to return again to the jail, hearing the solid, forbidding prison door swing shut behind him

with a sad and heavy thud. His days of imprisonment were – he hoped – over for good.

The Declaration of Indulgence gave Nonconformists the opportunity to apply for 'licences' so they could legally meet for worship. The Bedford congregation moved quickly to obtain one of these. In fact, they took advantage of the new ruling to purchase some land, buying an old orchard just off Mill Lane (now called Mill Street). The orchard contained a simple barn which they pressed into service as a ready-made meeting place. Both the barn and the orchard have long since disappeared, but 'Bunyan Meeting' continues to be based in Mill Street today. As well as obtaining a licence to hold services, it was also possible for individuals to get a 'licence to preach'. Indeed, a Nonconformist pastor without one of these would have risked immediate arrest. Much as Bunyan must have disliked having to do this, he asked for the required licence. This was granted on 9 May, that is, several months before he was formally pardoned! The times were chaotic and changes could happen in a rather odd order. There was a real risk the situation might turn again at any moment, with a new storm breaking over the Nonconformists. Nevertheless, by the second half of 1672, Dissenters enjoyed more liberty than at any time since the Restoration. Bunyan was determined to take full advantage.

A NEW MINISTRY

One of his first and most important moves was a strategic one, and relates to his application for a licence to preach. This application was actually part of a much larger document in his handwriting. The document requested licences not only for him but also for twenty-six other preachers. At the same time, the application sought to register twenty-nine meeting sites in addition to Mill Lane. Most of the sites were in Bedfordshire (for example, a licence was sought for a Meeting House in Newport Pagnell, where Bunyan had been stationed as a Parliamentary soldier), but others were in neighbouring counties, for instance Ashwell in Hertfordshire and Gamlingay in Cambridgeshire. Many of the churches that met in the different towns and villages enjoyed close, friendly relationships already. But the joint applications for recognition, clearly the result of prayer and discussion between the leaders of the different groups, further strengthened these links and helped to forge some new partnerships too. The applications were all successful. Now there was a ready supply of mutually recognised preachers, men that the churches could have confidence in and who would not – as long as the new situation held – be arrested for going about their work. Many of these preachers were more than willing to travel long distances, criss-crossing Bedfordshire and its adjoining counties to encourage smaller churches. This was especially important for some of the tiny groups geographically isolated in far-flung villages. This strategic approach enabled Dissenters in Bedford and the surrounding areas to support each other, with the strong helping the weak. With this new network to sustain them, Nonconformists in and around the Bedford district began to flourish.

Now he was no longer a prisoner, the travelling tinker was never going to be confined to one place

Bunyan was one of the preachers eager to visit other fellowships in addition to ministering in his own congregation. Even when he had been in jail he had somehow managed to make trips to London! Now he was no longer a prisoner, the travelling tinker was never going to be confined to one place. And the invitations to preach flooded in. True, he did not become nationally famous until after the publication of *The Pilgrim's Progress*. Although this was now substantially written, as we have seen it was kept back from the presses until 1678. But by the early 1670s he had certainly become something of a local celebrity. In fact, within a few years of his release he was being referred to as 'Bishop Bunyan' because of his standing among the churches. Given Bunyan's view on bishops he is unlikely to have been best pleased! As well as being a well-known figure in Bedfordshire, he was recognised in London too, certainly in Nonconformist circles. He developed friendships with other Dissenting pastors, for example, with the influential Puritan theologian and Congregational minister, John Owen. Bunyan the preacher was increasingly in demand.

He travelled widely, riding on horseback to take services as far afield as Leicester. We know he was there on Sunday 6 October 1672, because it is recorded he showed officials there his licence to preach. And it appears he was a regular visitor to a particular spot near Hitchin in Hertfordshire. About three miles outside the town there was some thick woodland within which there was an open patch of ground. The place was perfect for preaching, with gently sloping banks around the sides of the open area making it a sort of natural amphitheatre. Hundreds of people could gather in the open air for an outdoor service. Most could see the preacher clearly and, it appears, all could hear, indicating Bunyan must have had a strong, clear voice. The grassy clearing within the wood became known locally as 'Bunyan's Dell'. The location was perfect, not least because its relative isolation meant lookouts could be posted in the surrounding woodland to warn the worshippers if the authorities were approaching. If the pendulum swung again and persecution returned, such protection would become very important. Bunyan and his friends were only too aware this might happen. And their fears were about to be realised.

In 1673 Charles II's Declaration of Indulgence was withdrawn, less than two years after it had first been granted. What did this mean for Nonconformists? Confusion reigned. In particular, it was unclear whether licences already given to Dissenting preachers and congregations remained valid. Magistrates around the country took differing views. In Bedford, Bunyan was able to continue taking services and his church was able to continue meeting openly – for the moment. But from now on he in particular would have to take great care, especially when he was away from Bedford. Because of his growing reputation, he would be one of the first targets if the magistrates in a particular area decided now was the time to clamp down on those annoying Nonconformists. We can imagine the lookouts around Bunyan's Dell scanning the horizon anxiously whenever their favourite preacher was there.

THE AGNES BEAUMONT INCIDENT

Bunyan escaped re-arrest at this time, but he was unable to avoid a different sort of attack, one which caused him great distress. Unexpectedly, there was a danger he might become engulfed by scandal. This involved a woman called Agnes Beaumont, who was a member of the Bedford church (her name is written in the church book, in Bunyan's own handwriting, as 'Agniss Behement'). She was twenty-two years of age and unmarried, living in a small village called Edworth with her widowed father, John. The father had once shown some spiritual interest but by 1674 he had turned against the Bedford church and, in particular, had become an outspoken opponent of its new pastor. He often prevented Agnes attending services and there was clearly tension between the two of them. Agnes's brother, also called John, lived nearby and was much more sympathetic to Christian things than his father. He knew Bunyan, and often attended meetings of the church with his wife, although there is no evidence he ever became a member.

Agnes was an able, brave and godly young woman, who left her own account of the 'incident' which unfairly threatened both her and her pastor's reputation. According to her, in February 1674, Bunyan was due to take a service at Gamlingay where, as we saw, there was a licensed meeting place. Agnes was very keen to attend, as Gamlingay was only 7 miles from Edworth. Repeatedly she asked her father, who at last grudgingly gave his permission. But it was

Left:

Bunyan's

chair

cold and wet and the lanes that were the only route to Gamlingay, uneven at the best of times, were now particularly rutted and muddy. She would need a lift to the meeting, as it was judged too difficult a journey for her to take on foot. Her brother and his wife were planning to go, and they were using the only available horse. A man promised to take her, with Agnes 'riding pillion'; that is, sitting behind him. But although she waited patiently with her brother at the appointed time, the man in question failed to arrive. Agnes was thoroughly disheartened. It appeared she wouldn't be able to attend the service after all.

... but a local man accused Agnes of poisoning her father – at Bunyan's suggestion!

Then, unexpectedly, Bunyan himself rode into the village, passing through on his way to take the meeting! And he had no one with him! Perhaps he would give Agnes a lift? She was too shy to make this request herself, so brother John did so on her behalf. Initially, Bunyan refused. He knew full well what Agnes's father thought of him. And, although it was not so unusual for a woman to ride on horseback with a man, Bunyan judged it might leave him open to accusation. But soon both John and Agnes were pleading with the preacher. Eventually he gave way. This change of heart was, as it turned out, extremely unwise.

The local Anglican curate saw the two ride out of the village together, with Agnes sitting behind Bunyan with her arms around him. According to Agnes's own account, the curate looked at the two of them 'as if he would have stared his eyes out; and afterwards did scandalize us after a base manner, and did raise a very wicked report of us'. After the meeting she returned home with someone else, only to find that her father had heard the curate's 'wicked report'. He locked her out of the house, and she had to spend the night in a freezing barn. The father eventually forced her to promise that, while he was still alive, she would not attend any more of Bunyan's meetings. Only after she had reluctantly agreed to this cruel and high-handed demand was she allowed back into her home.

All of this would have provoked scandal enough for Bunyan. But there was a further twist to the tale. Within two days the father was dead. This appears to have been due to a heart attack, but a local man accused Agnes of poisoning her father – at Bunyan's suggestion! It appears the accuser's son had previously wanted to marry Agnes, only to be rejected by her. Here was a bizarre allegation made out of spite, with no evidence to support it. Agnes was cleared of murder, but the brave and pious woman continued to be subject to ridicule and unfounded accusations. As far as Bunyan was concerned, his reputation was in danger of being buried under the shower of mud hurled against him by his enemies.

He felt he had to defend himself in print. So, in a new addition of *Grace Abounding* he added some extra material, declaring that 'if all the … adulterers in England were hanged by the neck until they be dead, John Bunyan, the object of their envy, would still be alive and well'. There was more groundless gossip about him circulating. He was accused of being a witch (belief in witchcraft was rife in seventeenth-century England) or even a highwayman. He took the opportunity to deny these foolish rumours as well, insisting indignantly he was innocent of all the 'charges' against him. The fact he had denied the rumours so publicly showed he was worried though. Just because he had been released from jail did not mean his troubles were over. Indeed, worse was to come. The political situation was about to shift yet again. And when it did so, he would find his cherished freedom hanging by a thread.

RENEWED PERSECUTION

In February 1675, a clear ruling was given concerning the licences awarded under the old Declaration of Indulgence. They were all invalid. The last vestiges of Nonconformists' protection had now been stripped away. Magistrates were encouraged to prosecute, with those who had previously been lenient being told in no uncertain terms that this was their duty. There was to be a particular focus on those preachers who continued to take services. The network of Dissenters Bunyan had helped establish meant there was some organisation to help those fellowships in touch with the Bedford Meeting. But now any services had to take place in secret with the churches effectively going 'underground'. The prominent preacher, writer and ex-prisoner John Bunyan was especially vulnerable, as we've already noted. On 4 March a warrant was issued for his arrest. He had to decide what to do and, perhaps surprisingly, he chose to leave Bedford and go into hiding. Almost certainly he fled to London, where there was more chance he could remain undiscovered. Most importantly, Nonconformists were strong in the capital and by this time there were many who were friendly towards him who might give him shelter. But wherever he was, one thing was certain. Bunyan was a hunted man.

Why did he flee when earlier in his career he had faced the possibility of arrest squarely? In 1660 he had insisted on preaching at Lower Samsel even when the people there told him his arrest was imminent. What was different now? It is possible the years of squalid prison life – the loss of freedom, the cramped conditions, the stench, the threat of disease – had taken its toll. Perhaps, at least for a while, his nerve failed. If this were the case we could hardly blame him. But, most likely, his friends counselled him to go on the run, arguing little would be gained by his arrest. Conversely, if he remained free he could use his influence for good in London, returning to his home town when times were better. Certainly there is no censure of him in the Bedford church book, even though the new pastor was separated from his people. But whatever the reasons, he was now a fugitive. In a short work entitled *Instruction for the Ignorant*, written around this time, he spoke of being 'driven away' from his people.

Assuming Bunyan *was* in London then he was far from safe even there. The government had set up a system of informants who were handsomely paid for their work. These unscrupulous people received up to eight pounds if information they provided led to a conviction. This was a princely sum at the time, very tempting to

Right:
Bedford
Bridge today

the many Londoners who had spent the best part of their lives in grinding poverty. Godly men and women lived in fear. Could the person sitting next to them in their service actually be an informer? And who was that hammering on the door? Had their meeting been discovered and were the authorities about to burst in? It is hard for some of us to think of England as having been like this, a place of fear and suspicion where it was not possible to worship freely. But this was what 1675 and 1676 were like for many Nonconformists up and down the land.

To add to Bunyan's troubles, on 7 February 1676, his father, Thomas, died. To the end of his days he was working as a tinker, and he remained poor, leaving just a shilling each to his four children. As an illiterate he would not have been able to read his son's books and we do not know if he ever turned to Christ. Almost certainly John, still in hiding as if he were some notorious criminal, was unable to attend his father's funeral. The period of persecution showed no sign of abating and it would have been a massive risk for him to show his face in Bedford. He was not especially close to his father, but he was an emotional man who felt things deeply. We can imagine his distress.

IMPRISONMENT AGAIN

In December 1676, Bunyan made the momentous decision to return to Bedford. It is unclear why he did this. The campaign against people like him was intensifying, with increased use of surveillance. Some of the informants were convicted criminals, real lowlifes who would stop at nothing to trap a Nonconformist, thus reaping a financial reward. Possibly he thought his chances of remaining undetected were slim, even in London. Or perhaps he had just tired of his cloak and dagger existence, always being in hiding. What is certain is that he would have known his likely fate as he approached his old town. Once the authorities heard he was there, they wasted no time in moving against him. He was quickly arrested and imprisoned – possibly this time in the small lock-up on the old town bridge. Yet again there was no set length to his sentence. For all Bunyan knew, as a jail door closed on him once again, he might be in prison for the rest of his life.

During this second jail term, Bunyan put the finishing touches to *The Pilgrim's Progress* and kept in touch with his church. To begin with the situation looked grim but, mercifully, within six months he was free again. Some London contacts – including John Owen – had been able to speak to men of influence and arrange his release. This was all the more surprising as the situation generally was still hostile to Dissenters. In Bedford, Bunyan's church was again being persecuted, with members subject to further fines and confiscation of goods. The prisoner was free again, but for how long?

This chapter has seen Bunyan's fortunes ebb and flow. But overall, the time following his release had been personally difficult. What's more, true freedom of worship seemed more distant now than it had been at any time since the end of the Puritan Commonwealth. But it would be inappropriate to end this chapter on a downbeat note. Bunyan had used the opportunities he did have for effective gospel ministry. He had travelled widely and had been called as a pastor too. There had been much difficulty, but much effective ministry too.

GOING FURTHER

At this stage of his career, what was the message he preached, how did he preach it, and what effect did it have? One of Bunyan's shorter books, written in the period covered by this chapter and published in 1676, gives us important insights into his ministry. Entitled *Saved by Grace*, this was effectively an expanded sermon. It was material he had preached – probably in several places – and then written up for publication. This particular message was strongly doctrinal. It dwelt on some of the key truths of the Christian faith, such as the meaning of the cross. Some of its passages must have stretched the minds of his hearers and, later, his readers. By this time, Bunyan had spent many years reflecting on biblical truth, and he was an able theologian. Truth mattered, and Bunyan had given much time and thought to understanding it.

Yet what is especially striking about the sermon is the way biblical truth had gone deeply into his heart as well as his mind. He didn't just know about the cross, he gloried in it. Here was not just head knowledge but heart knowledge too, knowledge that affected his whole life. The following quotation is a particularly good example of how Bunyan was gripped with his message. He is speaking of how the cross is the place where God's grace is supremely shown.

> *Thou Son of the Blessed, What grace was manifest in Thy Condescension? Grace brought Thee down from Heaven; grace stripped Thee of Thy Glory; grace made Thee poor and despicable; grace made Thee bear such burdens of sin, such burdens of sorrow, such burdens of God's curse as is unspeakable: O Son of God! Grace was in all Thy tears; grace came bubbling out of Thy side with the Blood; grace came forth with every word of Thy sweet mouth ... Grace came out where the whip smote Thee, where the thorns prict Thee, where the nails and spear pierced Thee: O blessed Son of God! Here is grace indeed! Unsearchable riches of grace! Unthought of Riches of grace! Grace to make angels wonder, grace to make sinners happy, grace to astonish Devils!*

This was strong doctrine – about sin and, especially, the grace of God shown in the cross – which was deeply felt. This powerful, emotional passage is evidence of the full commitment of the preacher to his message. Bunyan spoke in such a way because he had experienced the grace of God personally and repeatedly.

Unsurprisingly, this sort of ministry was fruitful. Agnes Beaumont records her reflections of the service Bunyan took at Gamlingay like this:

> *Oh, I had such a sight of Jesus Christ that brake my heart to pieces. Oh, how I longed that day to be with Jesus Christ; how fain would I have died in the place, that I might have gone ... to him, my blessed Saviour. A sense of my sins, and of his dying love, made me love him, and long to be with him.*

It appears that at Gamlingay Bunyan also focused on Christ, His cross, and the grace which He pours into our lives, just as he did as he preached *Saved by Grace*. At Gamlingay Bunyan was able to draw Agnes, and doubtless many others, into a rich experience of God which paralleled his own.

 YOUR OWN JOURNEY

Bunyan's mature ministry gives us a pattern for engaging with God. We need to think clearly about our faith, growing in understanding of the great truths of the gospel. But it is not enough to know about Christian truths, even if we understand them well. The gospel needs to penetrate mind *and* heart, so that it becomes a part of us. 'Sound doctrine' should lead us to love God and others more deeply, more passionately. This is the pattern Bunyan gives us. We do well when we follow his example.

CHAPTER 9

TWO MORE STORIES:
The Holy War and
The Pilgrim's Progress:
Part 2

Samuel Sanderson

Joshua Symonds

Samuel Hillyard

John Jukes

John Brown

W. Charter Piggott

Ebenezer Chandler

William F. Coates

John Bunyan

Leonard Brooks

Samuel Fenn

C. Bernard Cockett

John Whiteman

Ralph H. Turner

John Burton

Leonard T. Towers

John Gifford

James W. Alexander

TO THE GLORY OF GOD AND IN COMMEMORATION OF THE TER-CENTENARY OF BUNYAN MEETING (1650-1950)

Evangelist (John Gifford, Minister 1650-55) points the way to Christian (John Bunyan, Minister 1671-88)

The
OLY-WAR
by John Bunyan.

THE
Holy War.

MADE BY
SHADDAI
UPON
DIABOLUS;

For the Regaining of the
Metropolis of the WORLD;
OR, THE LOSING
And Taking again of the Town
OF
MANSOUL

By *JOHN BUNYAN*, Author of the
Pilgrim's Progress, 1st. and 2d Parts.

Note. The 3d Part suggested to be his, is an Imposition.

I have used Similitudes, Hof. xii. 10.

GLASGOW,
Printed in the Year 1790.

I n the period following his release from prison, Bunyan continued to write. As we saw in the previous chapter, he produced a number of short books such as *Instruction for the Ignorant* (1675) and *Saved by Grace* (1676). But there were more ambitious projects too. After the publication of *The Pilgrim's Progress* in 1678, and its overnight success, there was huge interest in Bunyan as a writer. What would this gifted, original man come up with next? Growing in confidence, he was ready to try his hand at other allegories, and within the space of eight years three major works in this fresh, popular style appeared. His fertile mind was now working with astonishing speed and the ideas poured forth.

The first of these three books was *The Life and Death of Mr Badman*, published in 1680. It seems Bunyan meant this to be a sort of mirror image of *The Pilgrim's Progress*. Whereas Christian travels on an upward path towards the Celestial City, 'Mr Badman' is on a low road to hell. And while Christian grows in knowledge, love and faithfulness as his pilgrimage proceeds, Mr Badman's life gets progressively worse and more miserable as his behaviour spirals downwards. *Badman* was meant as a cautionary tale, a spiritual wake-up call for the ungodly, as well as a warning for Christians who were tempted to leave the pilgrim path. It is an extremely important work. Of all of Bunyan's books, this is the one which is most like a modern novel; in fact, some scholars regard it as the very first novel written in English. As such it is a major landmark in the history of English literature. But most agree it is not as satisfying as his earlier allegory (hardly surprising, given the rather depressing subject matter). At the time it was not especially popular. *The Pilgrim's Progress* went through eleven editions in the author's lifetime, whilst in the same period *Badman* was reprinted just once. If Bunyan had meant this new book to be a sequel to his

Left:

Eighteenth-century edition of *The Holy War*

earlier one then people were disappointed. It was relatively well received, but they wanted something else.

The next two allegories are much better known, and these are the books we will focus on in this chapter. The first of these is *The Holy War*, an ambitious, lengthy work, over 100,000 words in total. This was published in 1682. Amazingly, it was most likely written in less than a year. Of course, many of the ideas for the book would have been maturing in Bunyan's mind for a while. Perhaps the late 1670s and early 1680s were times of 'reaping' for him as a writer. Various 'seed thoughts' had been sown during his long prison years and had steadily grown. Now they were bearing fruit and ready to be harvested. But even if this is true, the pace at which he worked is quite astonishing, especially when all of his other responsibilities are taken into account. *The Holy War* is an epic story dealing with a host of weighty themes, for example, creation, the fall, salvation, growth into holiness and spiritual warfare. The allegory is intricate and multi-layered. Because of its complexity, some readers – both then and now – have made heavy weather of parts of it. The different strands of *The Holy War* do not always weave together as well as they might. Nevertheless, given the degree of difficulty of what was being attempted, the book still represents a tremendous achievement. Bunyan's ability to conjure up a scene and make it live using just a few well-chosen words and phrases is extraordinary. And, like the rest of his writing, the book has much to teach us about the Christian life.

THE HOLY WAR

The story centres around the town of 'Mansoul', which represents the human soul. The town is full of people such as 'Mr Conscience' and 'Captain Resistance' who stand for different dimensions of our personalities. As the book proceeds a long and bitter war is waged over Mansoul. This mighty conflict is between 'Diabolus', who represents the devil, and 'Shaddai', who represents God.

For Bunyan, this was the most important fight in the world. Indeed, it was more important than life and death itself, for it had consequences that would last for all eternity. How does the plot of *The Holy War* unfold? The original editions had no chapters; the book was one, long, continuous narrative, making it hard to navigate. After the author's death those who prepared new editions wisely broke the book up into different chapters. Perhaps the best way to approach *The Holy War* is to divide it into its key sections.

Section 1: Creation

At the beginning of the book, the original beauty of Mansoul is described. The town was built by Shaddai and is the pinnacle of all He had made, a place of privilege and joy, light and life. In the middle of Mansoul there is a Palace or Castle, 'famous and stately'. The marginal notes make it clear the Castle signifies the human heart. The fortified town has five gates, and these are most important to the story. They are 'Ear-gate', 'Eye-gate', 'Mouth-gate', 'Nose-gate', and 'Feel-gate'. These represent the five senses through which temptation might enter. If an assault is made on the town, it is through these gates the enemies will attack. As long as they remain secure Mansoul is safe. They certainly need to

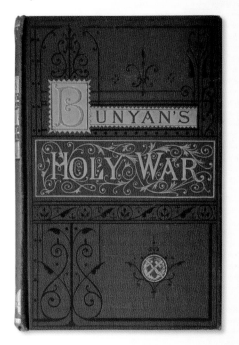

be closely guarded for the town has a dangerous enemy – Diabolus. We learn that he was once a 'great and mighty prince' and servant of Shaddai. But he rebelled against his rightful Lord and so was permanently excluded from His presence. He is clearly a foe to be reckoned with, but for the moment all is well in Mansoul, for it continues to live under the just and gracious rule of Shaddai. But Diabolus and his followers are watching on. And, ominously, they are busy scheming and plotting the town's downfall.

Section 2: Fall

Diabolus and his army march on Mansoul and soon the terrifying offensive begins. He chooses Ear-gate as the place to attack. But, rather than an all-out assault, he decides on a more subtle, indirect approach. He speaks to the people of the town, a clever address full of plausible sounding half-truths, as well as bare-faced lies and innuendo against Shaddai. To begin with he makes little impression. But then in a dramatic development Captain Resistance

is shot dead. As this important soldier topples to the ground from his vantage point on top of the wall, others in the town seem to lose the will to fight. As Bunyan puts it, 'poor Mansoul was wholly left naked of courage'. More smooth-talking follows and 'Lord Innocency', another important inhabitant of Mansoul, suddenly collapses. 'He sunk down in the place where he stood, nor could he be brought to life again.' As the 'Mansoulians' struggle in vain to revive him the horror of their situation strikes home: Lord Innocency too is dead. With these characters gone they weakly surrender. Both Ear-gate and Eye-gate are opened and Diabolus and his army march triumphantly in. The town is lost, despite hardly a shot being fired.

From this point, events move swiftly. Diabolus heads straight for the Palace – the heart – and takes control. His aim is to destroy all that is good in Mansoul with the help of his allies who enter with him, including a certain 'Mr No-Truth'. Books that contain the law of Shaddai are destroyed. A 'horrid and formidable' statue of Diabolus is set up in the town, and Mr No-Truth defaces all the images of Shaddai that he finds. It is important to note these images are defaced but not destroyed. Bunyan is making a theological point here. In the biblical Fall set out for us in Genesis 3, the image of God in men and women is badly marred but it is not completely destroyed. Human beings are still made in His likeness. Moreover, God still loves us despite our sin and rebellion, and longs to see His image fully restored in us.

The fact that Mr No-Truth is unable to completely shatter Shaddai's image is a sign of hope. Perhaps all is not lost in the town after all. Nevertheless, Mansoul is in a desperate state, as shown by the names of those chosen to govern it. They include, 'Mr Haughty', 'Mr Swearing', 'Mr Hardheart', 'Mr Pitiless', 'Mr Drunkenness', 'Mr Cheating', and 'Mr Atheism'. Others who are prominent in the town include 'Mr Lustings' and 'Mr Forget-good'. With characters like these in place, Diabolus feels secure. However, the story *The Holy War* tells has only just begun.

Section 3: Salvation

How will Shaddai respond to Diabolus's actions? The news of Mansoul's fall causes great grief to Shaddai and His Son, Emmanuel, but they are firm in their resolve. Mansoul will certainly be recovered again. Indeed, following this liberation, the town's condition will be even better than it was before it capitulated so feebly. We are told that the town's deliverance will be accomplished by the 'matchless love' of the Son, Emmanuel, who is also called the 'Prince'. He, of course, represents Jesus (see Isa. 7:14; 9:6; Matt. 1:23). The battle for Mansoul is on!

Shaddai marches on Mansoul with an army of 40,000 loyal fighting men, trained, equipped and ready for war. They have some success, but it is not until Emmanuel arrives with reinforcements that the battle turns decisively in their favour. Prince Emmanuel has brought with Him forty-four heavy battering rams and twelve huge slings so He can lay siege to Mansoul (these represent, as a marginal note tells us, the sixty-six books of the Bible). With such a formidable force now deployed against them, the town begins to weaken. Within the walls there are those, for example 'Mr Conscience', who urge the need for surrender. Now it is the Prince's turn to speak. In a powerful proclamation, He declares that Diabolus

Left:
Scene from
The Holy War

is a usurper who has no proper claim on the town. Mansoul belongs to Him and to Shaddai. First of all, they planned and constructed it. But also, we are told, Emmanuel has died for it. The cross is not at the centre of the narrative of *The Holy War*. It happens 'off stage' so to speak. We hear that Emmanuel's 'body' and 'blood' have been given for the town, and that amends have been made 'for its follies', but we never see this happen. Emmanuel's death is mysterious, and it is not really clear how it fits into the story, a weakness of *The Holy War*. But this much is certain: because Shaddai built the town and because Emmanuel has died for it then Mansoul is rightfully theirs — twice over. Diabolus has no right to inflict upon the town his cruel and tyrannical rule. His days in Mansoul are numbered.

The agonised wrestling … parallels Bunyan's own convictions and struggles prior to his own conversion

Bunyan describes the lead up to the battle and the action itself quite brilliantly. As he does so, he draws on memories of his former life as a parliamentary soldier. In *The Holy War* some of the troops carry pikes — long spears which were important weapons for infantrymen in the Civil War. His descriptions of infantrymen going through their drills — marching, wheeling around, standing to attention — is surely written with his own experiences at Newport Pagnell in mind. With his first-hand knowledge, his writing on military matters carries with it a clear note of authenticity. When the 40,000 march determinedly on Mansoul they have first to go through 'regions and countries of many people' in order to reach the town. Nevertheless, they pass through these without 'hurting or abusing' any people and they do not rob anyone of money or goods. This is in direct contrast with the conduct of troops in the Civil War — on both sides! Many of Bunyan's readers knew about the behaviour of different armies first-hand, how ill-disciplined, poorly-paid troops could ravage an area before moving on. An army arriving in your area were about as welcome as a plague of locusts, basically because they could be just as destructive. Bunyan was at pains to show that this was a different type of fighting force. Not only were they courageous in battle, ready to engage the 'cunning fox' Diabolus when the time came, but they were honourable and true in every way.

Bunyan's military scenes also draw on medieval imagery – the soldiers have swords, shields and helmets. And, above all, he draws from the Bible. These different influences come together to form a potent mix, enabling the author, with his extraordinary descriptive powers, to draw the reader into the heart of the battle. Readers experience the terror of the conflict, its sights, sounds and smells. Trumpets blare, drums beat and pipes play; colours unfurl and flutter in the wind; armour glitters in the sunlight. Under siege, the population of Mansoul becomes critically short of food. As famine sets in we feel the hunger with them. The heavy battle-slings 'whirl' large rocks into the town. There is 'hubbub' and 'tumult'; there are flames and thunderbolts.

The siege moves step by step towards its inevitable conclusion. A desperate Diabolus has put Mr Conscience in prison and convinced the people to 'harden their hearts' against the 'captains of Shaddai'. But as the siege intensifies they begin to waver. The agonised wrestling of the townsfolk parallels Bunyan's own convictions and struggles prior to his own conversion. As the fight unfolds, Ear-gate is once again crucial, for Bunyan believed that it was through hearing good preaching that conversion usually came. Finally,

> After three or four notable charges by the Prince and his noble captains, Ear-gate was broken open, and the bars and the bolts wherewith it was used to be fast shut up against the Prince were broken into a thousand pieces. Then did the Prince's trumpets sound, the captains shout, the town shake …

Ear-gate is open! Mansoul's liberation is at hand! Emmanuel and His forces stream into the town and take control. The townspeople know they deserve judgment and they tremble. Instead, they are shown great mercy. The Prince offers a 'large and general pardon'.

Still, some who tried to resist and have been taken prisoner by the attacking forces expect to die. They are taken to Emmanuel's camp with their 'feet in fetters'. They assume this is a prelude to their execution. But amazingly they are included in the gracious, wide-ranging pardon. They left Mansoul in chains and misery, but return with joy and with their 'steps enlarged'. What does Bunyan mean by this phrase? When prisoners were fettered their feet were often shackled closely together with a short length of chain, so they could only shuffle along with small, inhibited steps. But now their chains are off! Unencumbered, they can stride out freely. Bunyan's beautiful word picture dramatically encapsulates the joy of their unexpected, undeserved release. Here is wonderful mercy indeed.

Section 4: Discipleship and spiritual warfare

At this point the story could have ended. But Bunyan has much more he wants to say. Mansoul may once again belong to Shaddai and Emmanuel, but there is more work still to be done. Some of Diabolus's worst followers, for example Mr Atheist, have been put to death. But others still remain in the town, including the ominously named 'Mr Deceit', 'Lord Covetousness' and 'Lord Anger'. Emmanuel does not personally remain within the walls of Mansoul. Instead, He quits the town, leaving His court representative (signifying the Holy Spirit, who dwells in the hearts of all believers). Despite the court representative's presence, the town is suddenly besieged by an army of 'doubters'. It is not that Mansoul has ceased to be 'Christian'. Crucially, in the struggle that follows, the Palace or Castle, which we saw symbolises the human heart, always remains in the hands of Emmanuel's forces. But Mansoul is clearly finding it hard to live for its Prince.

For some readers, this might seem a surprising turn for the narrative to take. But Bunyan wants to emphasise not only the need for liberation – conversion – but also the importance of discipleship. Growth in holiness is crucial to him, as it was for all the Puritans. His continued use of the imagery of warfare is important here, for there is a spiritual battle which continues to rage long after someone has declared for Christ. I will say more about this in the 'Going further' section at the end of this chapter. Suffice to say here that spiritual warfare is one of the most important themes of *The Holy War*.

With the strength and power Emmanuel gives, this spiritual battle is gradually being won, step by painful step. Joy and peace begin to return to Mansoul. At the close of the book, Emmanuel gives a final speech to the townspeople. In the course of this He says,

> *Oh my Mansoul, I have lived, I have died, I live ... Because I live thou shalt live also. I reconciled thee to my Father by the blood of my cross, and being reconciled thou shalt live through me. I will pray for thee, I will fight for thee, I will yet do thee good. Nothing can hurt thee but sin; nothing can grieve me but sin.*

Emmanuel has returned, but Bunyan does not mean us to think this represents Christ's second coming. That event is still in the future. Indeed, there is a real sense in which the story of *The Holy War* is left unfinished. Even now, a few 'Diabolians' remain in the town, hoping for an opportunity to strike back. The victory is not quite complete. Again Bunyan wants to make an important point: no Christian is ever completely free from temptation, or indeed sin, in this life. But we are called to make progress in holy living and – thanks to God – such progress is gloriously, wonderfully possible. Jesus lives, and He prays for us and fights for us. Emmanuel's wonderful promise, 'Because I live thou shalt live also', is a promise for all of those 'Mansouls' who have yielded the 'Castle' of their hearts to Him. In other words, it is a promise for every Christian in every age.

THE PILGRIM'S PROGRESS: PART 2

When *The Holy War* appeared it was met with great acclaim and was widely read. On one level it was recognised as a wonderful adventure story; on another, deeper level, it gave much instruction and help for Christians. But, still, it wasn't *The Pilgrim's Progress*! Finally, the author bowed to pressure, putting pen to paper to write the sequel people really wanted. As with *The Holy War*, he again worked with remarkable speed, as vivid scene after vivid scene tumbled out of his well-stocked mind and onto the page. First published in 1684, *The Pilgrim's Progress: Part 2* centres on the story of 'Christiana', Christian's wife, telling how she became a follower of Jesus herself. Here was a worthy follow up to *The Pilgrim's Progress*. This new book showed conclusively that the earlier volume had been no fluke. His reputation as a writer was now secure.

The journey begins

The book opens with Christiana and her four children still living in the dreaded City of Destruction. But Christiana's attitude is now quite different to when we last met her. As she recalls her husband and his pilgrimage she feels broken and comes under spiritual conviction. She blurts out to her boys, 'Sons, we are all undone. I have sinned away your father, and he is gone; he would have had us with him; but I would not go myself; I also have hindered you of life.' The children start to weep. Bunyan skilfully paints a picture of hopelessness. All seems lost.

Yet then someone calls on the family. His name is 'Secret'. He comes in God's name and gives Christiana and her children an invitation to embark on pilgrimage, as Christian had done. Christiana is overwhelmed. Can it really be true? The man assures her it is; there is still a chance for her and her children. 'Secret' is one of the less obvious names in the allegory. Why does Bunyan give the godly messenger this name? Probably he has in mind the apostle Paul's description of the gospel as a 'mystery' – something which was hidden in times past but which is now revealed (Col. 1:26–27). In these verses Paul goes on to say that the mystery is 'Christ in you, the hope of glory'. Because of Christ, the family now have a hope and a future. Some of the family's neighbours – 'Mrs Inconsiderate',

Right:
Scene from
*The Pilgrim's
Progress: Part 2*

'Mrs Light-mind', 'Mrs Know-nothing', and the wonderfully named 'Mrs Bats-eyes' – hoot in derision and do their best to stop Christiana accepting the invitation. But, together with a young friend named 'Mercy', Christiana shuts her ears and resolutely leads her family away from the City and towards the Wicket Gate.

As they set off, Mercy says the following:

MERCY AT THE WICKET GATE.

Let the most blessed be my guide,
If't be His blessed will,
Unto His gate, unto his fold,
Up to His holy hill.

And let Him never suffer me
To swerve or turn aside
From His free grace, and holy ways,
What e'er shall me betide.

And let Him gather them of mine,
That I have left behind.
Lord make them pray they may be Thine,
With all their heart and mind.

The poem is effectively a prayer for God to guide her and to keep her faithful, so she can receive even more of His grace and grow in holiness. And she also expresses her desire for God to work in the hearts of those she has 'left behind'. May they become wholehearted pilgrims too! These are all good sentiments. We might not use the same seventeenth-century language, but the essential content of Mercy's prayer is good for any age, including today.

The band of pilgrims stagger through the Slough of Despond and manage to reach the Wicket Gate. Mercy is full of fear. She is the only one of the would-be pilgrims who does not have a direct invitation from 'Secret'. Perhaps her way will be barred and she will have to turn back, whilst the others go on? The prospect of this is too much for Mercy, who faints at the gate. But they are assured they are all welcome. Confessing their sin and receiving forgiveness, each one of them passes through. They are then lifted up to the top of the Gate, from where they can see the cross some distance away. This, they are told, is the means of their salvation. They will see the cross again as they journey on. As already noted, the death of Christ is not especially prominent in *The Holy War*, a criticism that has been justly levelled at the book. Here in *The Pilgrim's Progress: Part 2* the balance is redressed, for the cross is where it should be, centre stage.

The journey itself

As the little band press determinedly forward, they come upon many of the places and characters Christian encountered. They spend time in the Interpreter's House and of course pause at the cross; they tackle the Hill Difficulty, get past the lions and stay at the Palace Beautiful; and they learn, perhaps surprisingly, that Vanity-Fair has become more 'moderate'. Faithful's martyrdom has somehow shamed those who live there. Although there is no deep change in the people, they are at least a little more moral and restrained. Overall, while there is much in the story that is familiar, Christiana's experiences are different from her husband's. There are completely new characters too, for example 'Mr Great-heart' and 'Mr Honest'. Great-heart is especially important, for as well as being a pilgrim himself he acts as a guide and helper to Christiana and her group. When they reach Doubting-Castle, Great-heart and the other pilgrims battle against Giant Despair as they attempt to escape from his awful clutches. In a prolonged and desperate fight to the death, the Giant is surrounded by pilgrims trying to slay him. But still he survives having, as Bunyan puts it, as 'many lives as a cat'. Finally the terrible Giant is brought down, but still he stubbornly refuses to die. Yet Great-heart will not give

Left:

Scene from

The Pilgrim's

Progress: Part 2

up. Summoning his final reserves of strength, he at last finishes off his foe as he severs the Giant's head from his shoulders with a decisive stroke of his sword. Bunyan's own battles with despair were just as hard fought and hard won. When the victorious pilgrims subsequently demolish Doubting-Castle they find to their horror that the dungeon is 'full of dead men's bones'. Bunyan was grateful to be delivered from his own crushing despair, just as he was grateful for his release from Bedford Jail. Perhaps as he wrote about the skeletons in the castle's dungeon he thought of what his own fate might have been, and gave thanks to God.

Something so normal today was controversial in [the] seventeenth-century

Poetry and songs are important in *The Pilgrim's Progress: Part 2*. Bunyan may have included them because he wanted to encourage congregational singing. Something so normal today was controversial in seventeenth-century Nonconformist life. His own Bedford church was split on this issue and they did not officially allow hymn-singing until 1691, that is, after Bunyan's death. Their pastor, who loved music, was almost certainly frustrated by this stance! As already noted, *The Pilgrim's Progress: Part 2* contains the lines which were later adapted for the hymn, 'He who would valiant be', lines that are spoken, appropriately, by a character called 'Valiant-for-Truth'. At another point in the narrative, the travelling group all break into song together:

> *What danger is the pilgrim in,*
> *How many are his foes,*
> *How many ways there are to sin,*
> *No living mortal knows.*
> *Some of the ditch shy are, yet can*
> *Lie tumbling in the mire:*
> *Some though they shun the frying pan,*
> *Do leap into the fire.*

Bunyan's variation on the 'out of the frying pan into the fire' phrase might sound a bit of a cliché to us, but it would have been much fresher for his seventeenth-century readers (the saying did not originate with him though; it had been around for a while). His point, of course, is that people might avoid one potential pitfall – for example, a ditch – only to fall headlong into another – the mire. The song does not seem particularly encouraging! But it is realistic about life and the obstacles we face as Christians. Bunyan never failed to emphasise that the pilgrim pathway is a tough one, not for the faint-hearted. But at the same time it is immensely rewarding, and perhaps this is why the group can sing these lines not only 'trembling', but also full of 'joy'. As they stride purposefully along they know they are engaging in something challenging yet wonderful. And they also know God is with them every step of the way.

One of the great strengths of *The Pilgrim's Progress: Part 2* is the deep sense of community that develops amongst the increasingly close-knit travelling band. Christian often faced dangers alone, or perhaps with just one companion. But here there is a whole group journeying together: Christiana and her children, Mercy (who marries one of Christiana's sons, Matthew), Great-heart, Honest, Valiant-for-Truth, and others, like 'Mr Stand-fast'. They not only sing together but support each other in a myriad of different ways. A strong bond develops between them, a bond that is forged out of their common purpose and commitment to Christ. This is a vision of the Church as it should be. As Bunyan's most famous lines declare, they battle through all sorts of 'wind' and 'weather', facing 'lions' and fighting 'giants', each one of them labouring 'night and day to be a pilgrim'. Bunyan is sure that being an active part of a local church – whatever challenges this may bring – is indispensable if someone truly wants to be a faithful pilgrim.

Reaching the Celestial City

As the book draws to a close, Christiana is the first of the pilgrims to cross over the River of Death. She knows her time has come and in a moving scene blesses her children and the others who have by now become like family to her. She commands her sons to be ready to face death themselves and urges Valiant-for-Truth to watch over them. Mr Honest says he 'shall be glad to see that you go over the river dry-shod.' Christiana's response is full of faith, hope and courage: 'Come wet, come dry, I long to be gone; for however the weather is in my journey, I shall have time enough when I come there to sit down and rest me, and dry me.' Christiana knows the River of Death is likely to be difficult to negotiate. It seems to have the potential to overwhelm pilgrims, dragging them under. But Christiana is so focused on her destination that the river, although daunting, has ceased to become a major issue for her. Whether she gets across it with difficulty or with relative ease does not matter that much.

Sometimes, critics accuse Bunyan of treating his female characters as second class, weakly dependent on the men around them for instruction and assistance. But this is not fair. It is true that Christiana and Mercy receive much help from Great-heart, Valiant-for-Truth and others. But so do many of the male pilgrims, such as 'Mr Ready-to-halt' and 'Mr Despondency'. Both Christiana and Mercy are shown to be faithful disciples, outshining many of the men in wisdom, love, constancy, bravery and depth of faith. Here, at the end of the book, Christiana is still showing true commitment, facing death with a bright, unshakeable faith. In her final blessings she exhorts both Ready-to-halt and Despondency to rise above their names and be strong. She and her friend Mercy are true-hearted women of God, examples to Christian women – and men – today.

As Christiana approaches the river bank, her friends are all with her. Valiant-for-Truth plays 'upon the well-tuned cymbal and harp for joy'. On the far side of the river, the bank is full of horses and chariots waiting to carry her up to the gates of the City. As she wades into the water she turns and waves goodbye one last time, before plunging on. The last words she is heard to utter are, 'I come Lord, to be with Thee and to bless Thee.' Other pilgrims follow as they receive the summons. Ready-to-halt, who is disabled, discards

Right:
Bunyan's
collected
Works

his crutches because he knows that where he is going he will no longer need them. His last words are, 'Welcome life'. When it is Valiant-for-Truth's time to cross, he chooses a biblical quotation, saying, 'Death where is thy sting?' and, as he goes down deeper into the water, 'Grave where is thy victory?' (1 Cor. 15:55). One of Bunyan's best-known lines is reserved for this brave warrior, repeated at the funerals of many faithful Christians since. As Valiant-for-Truth presses forward, the narrator comments, 'So he passed over, and the trumpets sounded for him on the other side.'

The moving, sympathetic treatment of death and dying that Bunyan gives on these pages is, in my view, some of his finest work. The speech of Mr Stand-fast is the final one of the book. Amongst other things he says:

> I see myself now at the end of my journey, my toilsome days are ended. I am going now to see that head that was crowned with thorns, that face that was spat upon, for me. I have formerly lived by hear-say and faith, but now

I go where I shall live by sight, and shall be with Him, in whose company I delight myself. I have loved to hear my Lord spoken of, and wherever I have seen the print of his shoe in the earth, there I have coveted to set my foot too.

At the end of our life journeys, may you and I be able to say the same. And may we all face death having the same assurance that having crossed over, we 'shall be with Him'.

GOING FURTHER

Thinking back to the panoramic epic *The Holy War*, we can ask the question, 'What is its central theme?' There are many, but there is a good case for saying the most important is spiritual warfare. Not only does a battle rage for the 'heart' of Mansoul but, once this has been captured, fierce conflict continues as the town progressively rids itself of the Diabolians and the godly inhabitants become more and more prominent. Some readers find a number of scenes overly violent, for example, when some of the Diabolians are taken and crucified by other inhabitants of Mansoul. The key is not to see someone like 'Mr Lustings' as an actual person but as sin which needs to be decisively dealt with. The Bible urges us to 'put to death' whatever belongs to the sinful nature (Col. 3:5). Indeed, those who 'belong' to Christ Jesus have 'crucified' the 'sinful nature with its passions and desires' (Gal. 5:24). We are to do battle in the power of the Holy Spirit against all that is wrong in our lives, turning from this to the good, keeping 'in step' with the Spirit day by day (Gal. 5:25). If *The Holy War* is in places a violent book this is not because Bunyan is encouraging us to engage in physical warfare against those we disagree with! The conflict he is in interested in is *spiritual* and internal. We are called to win the battle for holiness, being the best we possibly can be for God.

Like *The Holy War*, the themes explored in *The Pilgrim's Progress: Part 2* are many and varied. Spiritual warfare is again to the fore, for example, in the pilgrims' grim battle to overcome Giant Despair. Also important is the call to be wholehearted for God. Characters such as Christiana, Mercy, Great-heart and Valiant-for-Truth all hold out to us a picture of vigorous Christian living. To be sure they are different from each other, with different gifts and strengths. But they are all exemplary pilgrims, examples for us to emulate today.

However, *The Pilgrim's Progress: Part 2* is also noteworthy for the way people with weaknesses, struggles and significant failings are sympathetically portrayed. Bunyan had a pastor's heart and he wanted to walk alongside those who for various reasons found the Christian life difficult. I think he shows more empathy for 'strugglers' in Part 2 of *The Pilgrim's Progress* than he had earlier done in Part 1. The way he writes about Mr Despondency and Mr Ready-to-halt are examples of this. Another character, one we have not yet mentioned, is 'Mr Fearing'. As befits his name, Mr Fearing went through his pilgrimage beset by terrible fears and anxieties. His deepest fear was that he would be rejected by God. But as Bunyan describes Fearing's tortuous journey he does so with great tenderness and care. There are some lovely touches, not least when he reaches the River of Death and faces this final challenge. When he sees there is no bridge over the river, Fearing is petrified. Surely he will drown in the act of trying to cross. Perhaps he has come all this way for nothing and will never see the face of his Lord. But as the trembling pilgrim steps out into the river, Great-heart notices something. The water level is lower than he has ever seen it before. Fearing is able to walk across quite easily, only just getting his feet wet! All is well at the last after all.

Bunyan's careful and sensitive portrayal of Mr Fearing's story reflects the way God deals with us when we struggle and stumble in our Christian walk. God knows just how much we can bear. Some, like Valiant-for-Truth can get through water that is almost head high; others can only cope with the shallows. This is true not only in death but in the other challenges Christian pilgrimage throws up too. If you see yourself in Mr Fearing, Mr Ready-to-halt, or Mr Despondency or perhaps in another of Bunyan's colourful cast of flawed Christian characters, then you can know that God understands, and will see you through.

 ## YOUR OWN JOURNEY

The different themes highlighted in the 'Going further' section – that of vigorous spiritual warfare and being the best we can for God on the one hand, and God's care of the weak and struggling on the other – might seem contradictory. But they are not, indeed, they are complementary. Certainly, we should look to be exemplary pilgrims from this point on in our lives, depending on God's Spirit. A Christian of a later generation than Bunyan, the nineteenth-century evangelist D.L. Moody, once said, 'The world has yet to see what God can do with a man completely given over to him. God grant that I might be that man.' Christiana, Great-heart and many other of Bunyan's pilgrims would have said a loud, whole-hearted, 'Amen'! But one sign of growth in grace and holiness is an increased willingness to take care of those who are struggling. This is a willingness that both Great-heart and Christiana show. And the reality is that all of us find our pilgrimage difficult at one time or another. We need to know God understands our fears and failings. He will surely challenge us, but we will not be tempted over and above what we can endure (1 Cor. 10:13). Whether we are 'Great-heart' or 'Fearing' or (most likely) a mixture of the two, God by His grace will see us through.

CHAPTER 10

THE FINAL JOURNEY

Samuel Sanderson
Joshua Symonds
Samuel Hillyard
John Jukes
John Brown
W. Charter Piggott
Ebenezer Chandler
William E. Coates
John Bunyan
Leonard Brooks
Samuel Fenn
C. Bernard Cockett
John Whiteman
Ralph H. Turner
John Burton
Leonard T. Towers
John Gifford
James W. Alexander

✠ TO THE GLORY OF GOD AND IN COMMEMORATION OF ✠
THE TER-CENTENARY OF BUNYAN MEETING (1650-1950)
Evangelist (John Gifford, Minister 1650-55) points the way to Christian (John Bunyan, Minister 1671-88)

he publication of the allegories *The Pilgrim's Progress* and *The Holy War* changed Bunyan's life. By the year 1684 he was known near and far. In his introduction to *The Pilgrim's Progress: Part 2* he tells us that Part 1 had been widely circulated – at home and abroad. In his own country it was talked about in towns and villages, streets and fields. Many who had been sceptical at first had grown to love it. Its appeal spanned the generations: it was devoured by young and old. Although it was especially loved by the poor, it was also read by the rich and well-to-do. People the length and breadth of the land were talking about Christian and his journey to the Celestial City. And – amazingly – the former tinker from Elstow had an international following. There was an American edition and translations into a number of European languages. Bunyan celebrated his triumph in verse:

In France and Flanders, where men kill each other,
My Pilgrim is esteem'd a friend, a brother.
In Holland too, 'tis said, as I am told,
My Pilgrim is with some worth more than gold.

We can forgive Bunyan for rejoicing so openly in print. He had had a tough life. Perhaps that was why, in a Europe full of uncertainty, instability and conflict his writing was so well liked. People identified with the characters whose highs and lows were described so vividly. He now had a genuine bestseller on his hands. We remember he made very little money from this extraordinary success. But still he was satisfied with the spiritual impact of his work. He did not know this at the time, but in 1684 he was not far from the Celestial City himself, for he was entering the last four years of his life and ministry. Would he know some peace and quiet in these final years? The answer is

Left:

Stained glass window depicting the River of Death and the Celestial City from *The Pilgrim's Progress* no! This closing period of his life would be as tempestuous and challenging as anything that had gone before. It would also be extremely fruitful in terms of ministry.

THE POLITICAL SITUATION

Charles II died on 6 February 1685. He had had at least eleven illegitimate children by a number of different mistresses, but none of these could inherit the throne and his actual wife, Catherine, was childless. Therefore upon his death Charles's younger brother, the Roman Catholic James, became king. Now it was the turn of the Anglicans to be alarmed. What would this mean for them? But James pledged to support the Church of England, despite his own Roman Catholicism. And persecution for Dissenters continued. Bunyan was free and many Nonconformist meetings were still held. Yet the situation was increasingly difficult, so that some of the bigger Dissenting churches decided to scatter and meet in smaller groups in private houses: coming together for one large service was considered just too risky. As if to confirm this, in February 1686, three Dissenting Meeting Houses in London were seized by the government, with no compensation given. One was turned into a hospital and, tellingly, the other two were used as makeshift barracks for soldiers, as extra troops were now needed to maintain order in the capital. The new king's regime was increasingly unpopular and rumours of plots against him were beginning to circulate. Despite stating his intention to protect the Anglican Church, there was widespread fear James would force his kingdom to become Roman Catholic again. Many Protestant Christians were nervously looking over their shoulders.

In the midst of this volatile situation, Bunyan continued to pastor, preach and write. One book written during this unstable, uncertain period was *The Saints' Knowledge of Christ's Love*. In this he sought to encourage and strengthen Dissenters who once again were under fire because of their faith. He fully acknowledged the problems they were facing. Nevertheless, he insisted, they should not be dragged down by them. They had two courses of action open to them. The first was simply to give in to despair. This would have been understandable, but wrong. The second option was to appreciate all the more the breadth and height and depth of God's love for them (Eph. 3:18). This second approach was the one Bunyan advocated, with all his heart. The more God's grace was understood and received, the more the attacks on them would be bearable. For, however great the 'rage of men', the love of God for those who trusted Him was greater still. The persecution they were enduring was real, indeed, it seemed relentless. But God was with His people, and He would carry them through.

The early plots to overthrow James had been ruthlessly crushed, with the main leaders executed. Some Dissenters had been involved in these planned uprisings and others had been very sympathetic towards the plotters. Bunyan himself did not support violent revolution. In *The Saints' Knowledge of Christ's Love* he insisted kings and magistrates had been given their power by God (Rom. 13:1). But he was equally clear their power was limited for they only held it for as long as God allowed. If they behaved badly (and Bunyan was quite clear the king and his advisors were doing so) they would leave themselves open to terrible divine judgment. He daringly hinted God could replace a corrupt, ungodly regime with a new one whenever He chose. Bunyan's overarching point was that God was in control. He is always sovereign and works things out for the good of His people. They could trust in Him.

> *He daringly hinted God could replace a corrupt, ungodly regime with a new one whenever He chose*

Persecuted Nonconformists did not get to read *The Saints' Knowledge of Christ's Love* in 1686, the year we might reasonably have expected it to have appeared. Probably, potential publishers decided the political comments – subtle though they might have been – were just too dangerous to print. In a London seething with discontent and rumours, both publisher and author could easily have been locked up or worse. The manuscript was not published until after Bunyan's death.

THE SITUATION CHANGES

As 1686 wore on, persecution of Nonconformists became less intense. James, who was deeply disliked by many, had decided to change tack. Now there was increasing toleration for both Dissenters and Roman Catholics. On 4 April 1687 a new 'Declaration of Indulgence' was issued. There was freedom of worship as long as gatherings were peaceful and did not ferment revolution. Perhaps surprisingly, this did little to placate people. The Church of England leaders were unhappy because James seemed to be undermining and

Dr. Thomason Book

THE

Water of Life:

OR, A

DISCOURSE

SHEWING

The Richnefs and Glory of the Grace and Spirit of the Gofpel, as fet forth in Scripture by this Term, *The Water of Life.*

By *JOHN BUNYAN.*

And whofoever will, let him take the Water of Life freely, Revel. 22. 17.

LONDON,

Printed for *Nathanael Ponder,* at the

downgrading their privileged position. But many Dissenters were wary too. There was a widespread feeling that this Declaration of Indulgence was actually a cover, and that James's long-term objective was to re-establish Catholicism as the state religion of his realm, with people compelled to worship in that way. To cap it all, James seemed to want absolute power. The Declaration of Indulgence had been issued without reference to Parliament. Did James want to rule on his own as his father had sought to do, sparking the devastating Civil War? It seemed so. James's unpopularity continued unabated.

How would Nonconformists respond to the developing situation? A number of Dissenting churches sent 'addresses' to James — written statements of thanks for the toleration his 'Indulgence' seemed to promise them. Others dared to be openly critical of the king. As for the Bedford Meeting, there is no evidence they sent a positive address to James, but there is no evidence they actively opposed the Indulgence either. At least some in the Meeting took the opportunity toleration created to take some public role in the affairs of their town, something that would have been almost impossible previously. Probably they were neutral about what was happening. Certainly they would have been cautious. Freedom of a kind had come, but at what price and for how long?

THE WATER OF LIFE

Through all of this, Bunyan continued to preach and write. In fact, if anything, he increased the pace at which he worked. In the years 1687–88 he wrote probably ten new books, five of which were published in 1688, the year of his death. It has to be said that some of these were printed sermons, only lightly adapted before being sent to the publishers. Even so, his output was tremendous, a clear testament to his continuing energy and desire to be useful in God's service. He had been called to preach and write and that was what he was going to do, with all of his might! The five books published in 1688 are also evidence of the high demand there now was for his work. His sermons

Left:

A first edition copy of *The Water of Life*, published in 1688 and popular pamphlets were eagerly purchased and put alongside the longer allegories. Publishers now knew they were guaranteed brisk sales for anything which bore the name 'John Bunyan'.

One of the printed sermons which appeared in 1688 was entitled *The Water of Life*. Bunyan had taken as his text Revelation 22:1, 'And he shewed me a pure river of water of life, clear as crystal, proceeding out of the throne of God and of the Lamb' (AV). In this short but wonderful book a number of the key themes of his ministry come together.

First of all, the message highlights Bunyan's delight in biblical imagery. He loved the way the Bible uses metaphors and images to help us appreciate more deeply the wonders of God and His gospel. In *The Water of Life* he focuses on how the Scriptures use the image of water to depict God's amazing grace. Revelation 21 describes an abundant free-flowing river, pure, bright and clear. This, Bunyan says, sets forth to us the nature of God's grace, which is similarly excellent and life-giving. In his popular style, he contrasts 'the water of life' with the stagnant, putrid ponds and cisterns which would have been all too familiar to his readers, whether they lived in town or country. Unlike these festering, disease-ridden pools, the perfectly pure water of God's grace brings life instead of death. A wonderfully attractive picture of the grace of God is built up as Bunyan warms to his theme.

> *The free offer of the gospel to all people is something the mature Bunyan always emphasised*

Secondly, the sermon is full of God and gospel, something that is typical of Bunyan. As he revels in the biblical imagery, he declares it is God who is the glorious 'head or well-spring' of the water of life. Bunyan concentrates especially on Christ, the Lamb of God, for his text declares that it is 'out of the throne of God and of the Lamb' that the river flows. The description of Christ as the 'Lamb' points us to His death for, as Bunyan says, this picture shows us 'Jesus as sacrificed, Jesus as ... suffering'. It is through the cross of Christ that grace flows down to all those who put their faith in Him. The author was very much aware that the grace which is wonderfully free to us was infinitely costly to God. He glories in the gospel, and gives thanks to God for the wonderful love that was shown to us on the cross.

Thirdly, Bunyan wants to stress that all could come and receive this grace. On the title page of *The Water of Life* are printed the words of another verse in Revelation 22. This is verse 17, which reads: 'And whosoever will, let him take the water of life freely' (AV). The free offer of the gospel to all people is something the mature Bunyan always emphasised, and with great passion. Remembering his own doubts and struggles, as chronicled in *Grace Abounding*, he once again shows his keenness for others not to spend years in such doubt and despondency, wondering if the gospel is really for them. As he had made clear in *The Pilgrim's Progress*, no one who came to the 'Wicket gate' earnestly seeking God's forgiveness would be turned away. In this new work he makes this point yet again, but in a different way: the 'water of life' is available to all without exception.

Finally, he emphasises God's grace streams down to Christians throughout their lives, not just at the point of conversion. In a powerful passage he declares:

> *Grace can justify freely,* when *it will,* who *it will, from* what *it will.* *Grace can continue to pardon, favour and save* from *falls,* in *falls,* out *of* *falls. Grace can comfort, relieve and help those that have hurt themselves.* *And grace can bring the unworthy to glory.*

Grace certainly justifies sinners, making them right with God. However bad someone might be, however terrible their rebellion against God, they are fully forgiven when they trust in Him. But important as this is, Bunyan's primary emphasis in this extract is on grace for those who are already on the Christian journey. There is continued pardon, favour and salvation. We are saved from many falls, and even when we do trip over God is still with us to pick us up and lead us on. Grace comforts, revives, relieves and helps. And grace brings the unworthy believer through to final glory. By His grace He keeps a firm and loving hold on His people through all of the different 'seasons' of their lives. 'Grace abounding' had become the keynote of Bunyan's ministry. May we all know God's grace in our lives day by day as we journey on with Him.

Bunyan's text for *The Water of Life*, Revelation 22:1, is, of course, from the very last chapter of the Bible. Little did he know, but as he submitted the book for publication he was beginning the final chapter of his own life too. He had written much about how God sustained his children as they took the final steps of their earthly pilgrimage. What he knew by faith was about to be confirmed in his own experience.

JOHN BUNYAN'S DEATH

Bunyan was working right till the end. In August 1688 he completed another book, entitled *An Acceptable Sacrifice*, and prepared to set off for London for a preaching engagement. But before he did so he received a further request. Would he be willing to stop off at Reading on a mission of mercy? One of Bunyan's friends had quarrelled and fallen out with his father, who lived there. So sharp was the disagreement between the two men the father was threatening to disinherit the son. Would Bunyan be willing to try and mediate? Reading was not on the direct route from Bedford to London (the detour would increase the length of the journey by about a half). But, typically, Bunyan was willing. In mid-August he said goodbye to Elizabeth, saddled up his horse and set off.

The visit to Reading was a success. The respected John Bunyan was able to intercede on his friend's behalf, and the grounds were laid for a full reconciliation between father and son. Bunyan rode on, no doubt buoyed up by his success. But the increased journey time was to have fateful consequences. On the final leg of his journey to London, he was caught in a violent summer storm. Rather than seeking shelter he rode on. Buffeted by the wind and rain he was soon

Left:

John Strudwick's house where Bunyan died

soaked through. As a result of this he caught what early biographers described simply as a 'fever': perhaps pneumonia, perhaps influenza. His vigorous constitution had been weakened by years of travelling in all weathers, not to mention the ravages of his time in prison. Nearly sixty years of age, he was unable to throw off the illness.

He was still well enough to fulfil his preaching engagement, giving a sermon to a Dissenting congregation which met in Boar's Head Yard, near Petticoat Lane. This was later published as *Mr John Bunyan's Last Sermon*, probably based on notes taken by someone who heard him. It is not vintage Bunyan – perhaps the note-taker lacked skill, or perhaps the illness had already caught significant hold and the preacher was struggling. After the service, Bunyan returned to the house where he was staying on Snow Hill, in busy, bustling Holborn. This belonged to John Strudwick, who ran a grocer's shop from the ground floor of his narrow four-storey home. Strudwick and his family were fellow Dissenters and had become firm friends. Despite being in the care of good people, Bunyan's health began to deteriorate rapidly. He was slipping away.

Accounts of his death often owe more to imaginative reconstruction than hard evidence. Biographers sometimes draw from a document entitled *Mr John Bunyan's Dying Sayings*, but there is real doubt about the reliability of this, especially as no one knows who compiled it. It is full of extensive, carefully-phrased reflections on a wide range of topics, including prayer, worldliness, the nature of heaven and even Sunday observance. At one point Bunyan is recorded as saying, as he speaks about the life to come:

> *How will the heavens echo of joy, when the Bride, the Lamb's wife [that is, the church], shall come to dwell with her husband forever. Christ is the desire of nations, the joy of angels, the delight of the Father; what solace then must that soul be filled with, that hath the possession of Him to all eternity?*

parents and custody of any
To have and to hold a
and all other the afor
my wife her Executors
proper use and
of challenge
John Bunyan or of any
his my name
without any mon
done unto new
administrators or
singular the
Elizabeth my wife
the afore
before by the
the said John
my wife, in
singular the afor

These are great words, but they do not sound as if they come from a man about to take his final breath. Perhaps they were spoken before the illness had really become severe. Yet the reality is that little can be said with certainty about his last days. Early biographers were even confused about the date that he died, but this is now firmly established as Saturday 31 August 1688. On this day, miles from his beloved Elizabeth, John Bunyan finally crossed the river of death. 'And all the trumpets sounded for him on the other side.'

AFTERMATH

When Bunyan's Bedford congregation heard the news they were grief stricken. The church book says the following:

> *Wednesday 4th of September was kept in prayer and humiliation for this heavy stroke upon us, the death of dear brother Bunyan. Appointed also that Wednesday next be kept in prayer and humiliation on the same account.*

Their pastor was not buried in Bedford, but in London. This was in a cemetery called Bunhill Fields, where many prominent Dissenters have been laid to rest, both before and since his time. His funeral was on 2 September. It is unlikely Elizabeth was able to attend, indeed it is possible news of her husband's death did not reach Bedford until after the burial had taken place. The funeral would have been a modest affair. His body was interred, as was his Saviour's, in a 'borrowed tomb' – the Strudwick family vault. Bunyan left goods worth just over 42 pounds to Elizabeth. By contrast, his friend John Owen, who had died five years earlier and is also buried in Bunhill Fields, left an estate that was valued at over 2,000 pounds. Far more precious than Bunyan's property were his unpublished manuscripts, including *The Saints' Knowledge of Christ's Love*. These Elizabeth entrusted to one of her husband's London friends, Charles Doe, for publication. They helped cement and further develop his reputation as an author. In time Bunyan

Left:
Facsimile of
Bunyan's will

would outstrip all of those buried alongside him — including Owen — in terms of influence.

Elizabeth died only a few years later, in 1691. But she had lived to see what her husband did not — a decisive end to the worst of the persecutions. King James's reign came to an end just a few months after John Bunyan's death. A group of prominent Protestant noblemen had decided to act. There was a Dutch prince, William of Orange, who was married to one of James's daughters, Mary. William was staunchly Protestant and through marriage had a genuine claim to the throne. The noblemen invited William to come to England with an army and take control. All previous plots had failed, but this one was different. William landed on 5 November at Torbay in Devon and met little opposition. Some of James's leading officers chose this moment to switch sides and William was able to enter London in triumph without having to fight a battle. James attempted to flee but was captured, only to escape and make it across the water to France. William III and Mary II were declared joint sovereigns of England and Wales on 13 February 1669, and on 11 May of Scotland too. A new era had begun.

A 'Declaration of Rights' was issued which limited the powers of the monarchy and increased those of Parliament. Britain was now on the road to the 'constitutional monarchy' we have today. Even more important to our story is the 'Act of Toleration', passed on 24 May 1669. This allowed freedom of worship to Nonconformists. True, there were still restrictions and there was still discrimination against them (no Dissenter was allowed to attend university, for example). But compared to what had gone before, this seemed like real freedom. Looking back on this time a few years later, the eighteenth-century London Baptist Benjamin Wallin exulted, 'The Most High sent the glorious King William the Third, and saved us.' This was typical of the reaction of Nonconformists, especially as they became convinced that toleration was here to stay and not just a passing phase. The 1669 Act of Toleration is an important milestone in British religious history. For Nonconformists the period of intense persecution that had seen men like Bunyan harassed and hunted for much of their lives was over. In 1669 a new chapter in their journey as Christian people was beginning, but they would embark on this new era without one of their best-known and best-loved men.

GOING FURTHER

How might we assess the life of John Bunyan? On one level, it might be considered a sad life, even a failure. He spent over twelve years in prison. Even when he was free, he always had to be careful. Often persecuted, often on the run, regularly separated from his dearly loved wife and children, Bunyan knew little of the earthly security many of us take for granted. He made little money. Although he moved on from the oppressive poverty of his life in Elstow, the tinker turned writer/preacher made only a relatively small financial gain from his books. Indeed, in this area he suffered great injustice, as many unscrupulous publishers became well-off thanks to unlicensed editions of his works. Also, he struggled with depression for significant periods of his life. Although he knew greater peace in later years, the 'iron of melancholy' (as one writer put it) left a permanent mark on him. Finally, he died just before the persecution he and his friends had had to endure ended. Humanly speaking, surely this was a tragedy. So – viewed from this purely 'earthly' point of view – Bunyan's life seems a sad one.

Yet I am convinced this is not how Bunyan would want us to remember him. Some pursue wealth, comfort and ease, and earthly safety at any price. He was not one of those people. He was never wealthy in earthly terms, but his focus was on spiritual wealth – 'treasure in heaven' (Matt. 6:20). He was genuinely more concerned about helping people grow closer to Christ through his ministry than he was about making money; more interested in spiritual prosperity than material prosperity. He was never comfortable. His was a courageous life; it had to be, given the times he lived in and all he faced. But he was a man of principle, with unshakeable, deep convictions he was determined to live by come what may. At almost any time during his long imprisonment he could have been released – if he had sacrificed his principles. However, he steadfastly refused to do so. The battles he faced shaped him and fitted him for useful service. As a result he gained immense respect and was able to lead people through extraordinarily difficult times with vigour, integrity and grace.

Most of all, although earthly safety constantly eluded him, he knew he was eternally secure. At one time, his greatest fear had been God might not love him personally. Once he knew for sure Jesus was his Saviour, then he could face anything and everything knowing he was held in the strong and loving grip of his God. So, even before we reckon with the extraordinary legacy of his writings, Bunyan's life was a wonderful one. It was not primarily sad and even less was it a failure. Life lived for Jesus Christ never is. Bunyan put faithfulness to Christ over and above every other concern. Now he is with his Lord and knows his true reward.

 ## YOUR OWN JOURNEY

What will *our* lives count for? How might they be assessed? We could aim for comfort and ease in this life, sit lightly to principle and pursue financial wealth as our fundamental goal. Many do this, and if we follow their example then people might look at us and regard us as 'successful'. But it is not their assessment which matters. Bunyan's life challenges us to put faithfulness to God and His calling on our lives first, no matter what it costs us. As we seek to be men and women of principle, loving God and loving and serving others, we can expect many hardships. But Bunyan also knew great joy and purpose in life, and we can expect to know these things too. And of course one day we will see the Lord too. When we see Christ, like the subject of this biography, we will know our real reward, even treasure in heaven.

CONCLUSION:
THE INFLUENCE OF
JOHN BUNYAN

Samuel Sanderson
Joshua Symonds
Samuel Hillyard
John Jukes
John Brown
W. Charter Piggott
Ebenezer Chandler
William J. Coates
John Bunyan
Leonard Brooks
Samuel Fenn
C. Bernard Cockett
John Whiteman
Ralph H. Turner
John Burton
Leonard T. Towers
John Gifford
James W. Alexander

✠ TO THE GLORY OF GOD AND IN COMMEMORATION OF ✠
THE TER-CENTENARY OF BUNYAN MEETING (1650-1950)
Evangelist (John Gifford, Minister 1650-55) points the way to Christian (John Bunyan, Minister 1671-88)

V

続・天路歴程
天を目指す走者
バニヤンの言葉

ohn Bunyan's life was one of many journeys. He regularly travelled from place to place as a tinker and as an itinerant preacher. We can picture him striding purposefully across muddy fields or riding along narrow, treacherous country lanes. He was a man of vigour and action, often on the move. This was just one of the reasons why his long years of imprisonment were so tough. His extraordinary life was a journey in itself. He had been a blasphemer and a rogue but he had found Christ and been transformed. He was only 'a tinker and a poor man', as Elizabeth Bunyan memorably put it but, thanks to his Saviour, he also became a preacher, pastor and writer. And, of course, his most famous book was all about a journey. Perhaps *The Pilgrim's Progress* is so powerful and convincing because Bunyan himself knew the pilgrim life so well.

After his death, there is a sense in which the journey continued, for his books travelled the world over, known and treasured on every continent, passed on from father to son and mother to daughter as precious possessions. *Grace Abounding*, *The Life and Death of Mr Badman*, *The Holy War* and many of his other, shorter books have more than stood the test of the time. But it is the enduring success of *The Pilgrim's Progress, Parts 1 and 2* which would have simply staggered the tinker from tiny, rural Elstow. By 1700, twenty-two editions of *The Pilgrim's Progress* had been printed in English and by 1800 this number had risen to seventy. Yet it was the nineteenth and early twentieth centuries which saw the real explosion of its popularity so that, by 1938, an amazing 1,300 different editions had appeared. This last figure is all the more extraordinary because it does not include any foreign language translations. *The Pilgrim's Progress* has been published in over two hundred different languages and dialects, including Polish, Yoruba, Xhosa, Fanti, Basa and Mandarin.[12] The book has been simplified

Left:

Japanese edition of *The Pilgrim's Progress*

for children, abridged, turned into verse and adapted for the stage, most recently by the Saltmine Theatre Company. As already noted, it is the world's second most published book behind the Bible. Bunyan would certainly not want his work to rise any higher in the bestselling list! For him, the Scriptures were always primary.

Some have continued to look down their noses at Bunyan, deriding his popular, colloquial style. But, interestingly, many of the literary élite have now been won over. Every month there are new scholarly articles written on some aspect of Bunyan and his writings, with *The Pilgrim's Progress* once again taking pride of place. This man with so little formal education himself is now studied in detail in universities and colleges the world over.

Countless individuals have been influenced by him, many of them famous themselves. Vincent van Gogh, the brilliant Dutch painter once said, 'John Bunyan's *The Pilgrim's Progress*, Thomas à Kempis and a translation of the Bible; I don't want anything more.'[13] C.H. Spurgeon was hugely indebted to Bunyan. He described *The Pilgrim's Progress* as the 'sweetest of all prose poems' and made a gift of the book to Susannah Thompson, the woman who later became his wife, writing in the front of his 'desires for her progress in the blessed pilgrimage'. Terry Waite, the former peace envoy who was taken hostage in 1987 and held in Beirut, was influenced by Bunyan's example more than his books. Whilst he was being held in solitary confinement he received a postcard of one of the stained-glass windows at Bunyan Meeting, one which shows Bunyan in Bedford Jail. This, said Waite, gave him much needed hope and inspiration. Van Gogh, Spurgeon and Terry Waite stand as examples of the many different and diverse figures Bunyan has impacted. His influence is not only broad but deep.

Most people have heard of Van Gogh, and many of Spurgeon and Terry Waite. But just as important are those around the world who were never well-known whose lives have been significantly shaped by his books and his life. I think Bunyan would have been especially happy to know he had influenced so many 'ordinary' people. He

Right:
Foreign language editions of *The Pilgrim's Progress*

always championed the poor, oppressed and marginalised. In his books the heroes are usually working people. Even the captains of Shaddai's army in *The Holy War* are 'stout and rough-hewn men'. Truly he was the 'people's pilgrim', a man who encouraged and inspired those from all walks of life and backgrounds, especially the disadvantaged.

And has his influence ended? I hope not, for his life and writings have the potential to help equip a new army of so-called 'ordinary people'. These are people who will receive God's abounding grace, pray in the Spirit, engage in spiritual warfare and live the life of faithful pilgrims, followers of Jesus Christ who is the same 'yesterday, today and forever' (Heb. 13:8). God calls us to be 'Christians' and 'Christianas', 'Great-hearts' and 'Evangelists'. If we heed and follow this call then Bunyan's influence will live on and the journey will continue.

ACKNOWLEDGEMENTS

The experience of writing *John Bunyan: The People's Pilgrim* has been a wonderful one, made all the more positive by the different people who have journeyed with me as I have worked on the book.

Anthony Cross, Crawford Gribben, Judy Powles, Ian Randall and Emma Walsh all gave advice during the initial stages of research, pointing me to some really helpful resources which got me started. Much of this early work was undertaken during a three-month sabbatical from my teaching duties at Spurgeon's College. I am grateful to the Governors of the College and our Principal, Nigel Wright, for granting me this time, and to one of our students, Jon Law, for breaking into my sabbatical to suggest *The People's Pilgrim* as a potential title. Spurgeon's has become an increasingly special place for me because of the lively evangelical faith it embodies and because of the warm friendship of both staff and students.

Lindsay Caplen, Emma Hunnable, Vicky Martin and Tim Moyler all read draft chapters and told me they thought I was on the right track, as well as making some wise suggestions. A number of people connected with the Bunyan Meeting and Museum in Bedford have given invaluable help. Many of the illustrations in *The People's Pilgrim* have been taken from there and I am very grateful for the access and encouragement they have given. I warmly recommend a visit! I want to thank Chris Damp, Cherry Protheroe, Nicola Sherhod and, especially, Ruth Broomhall, a postgraduate student at Spurgeon's who lives in Bedford and has been closely involved with both the Meeting House and Museum for a number of years. She read and commented on the whole of the draft manuscript and helped me in numerous other ways too. Other illustrations are from the Saltmine Theatre Company's excellent production of *The Pilgrim's Progress*, and are used with permission.

The great team at CWR have given tremendous support. I am particularly indebted to Lynette Brooks, Director of Publishing, and to Mike Henson who worked so hard on the design and illustrations. Charlotte Hubback, the book's editor, commented on the text with great thoroughness and made many helpful and affirming comments. Thank you. Any errors and imperfections which remain are of course my own responsibility. Our children, Rachel and Joe, have regularly told me not to write something 'boring'. I hope I have succeeded; I know they'll tell me what they think! I value their friendship and encouragement more than I can say.

ENDNOTES

1. Adaptation by P.W. Dearmer (1867–1936). In the public domain.

2. There were Dutch and Flemish congregations in sixteenth-century London who practised believers' baptism, but they spoke their own languages. Persecution soon wiped out these churches.

3. I am drawing this information from V. Evans, *John Bunyan: His Life and Times* (Dunstable: The Book Castle, 1988) p.23. The rector whose horse came to worship was based at Carlton, near Bedford.

4. For a helpful explanation of these difficult verses, see J.R. Edwards, *The Gospel According to Mark* (Grand Rapids, Michigan: Eerdmans, 2002) pp.123–24.

5. R. Greaves, *Glimpses of Glory: John Bunyan and English Dissent* (Stanford University Press: Stanford, California, 2002) p.38. For the full discussion of Bunyan's psychological state, see pp.35–44.

6. I have contrasted the Puritan and later evangelical views on assurance in more detail in P.J. Morden, *Communion with Christ and his People: the Spirituality of C.H. Spurgeon* (Oxford: Regent's Park College, 2010) pp.70–76.

7. Corrie Ten Boom, *The Hiding Place* (London: Hodder, 1971) p.217. The words were spoken by Corrie's sister, Betsie.

8. For the argument that Bunyan must have been in the larger county jail, see J. Brown, *John Bunyan: His Life, Times and Work* (London: Hulbert, 1928) pp.151–53.

9. Love Maria Willis (1824–1908). Words in the public domain.

10. For example, The Barnabas Fund and Open Doors. See www.barnabasfund.org and www.opendoorsuk.org

11. C.S. Lewis, *On the Incarnation* (New York: St. Vladimir's Seminary Press, 1993 [1944]) p.4.

12. For more on the global reach of *The Pilgrim's Progress*, see I. Hofmeyer, *The Portable Bunyan: A Transnational History of* The Pilgrim's Progress (Princeton: Princeton University Press, 2004).

13. Thomas à Kempis was a fifteenth-century Christian who wrote the classic work of spirituality *The Imitation of Christ*.

Courses and seminars

Publishing and new media

Conference facilities

Transforming lives

CWR's vision is to enable people to experience personal transformation through applying God's Word to their lives and relationships.

Our Bible-based training and resources help people around the world to:
• Grow in their walk with God
• Understand and apply Scripture to their lives
• Resource themselves and their church
• Develop pastoral care and counselling skills
• Train for leadership
• Strengthen relationships, marriage and family life and much more.

Our insightful writers provide daily Bible-reading notes and other resources for all ages, and our experienced course designers and presenters have gained an international reputation for excellence and effectiveness.

CWR's Training and Conference Centres in Surrey and East Sussex, England, provide excellent facilities in idyllic settings – ideal for both learning and spiritual refreshment.

CWR Applying God's Word
to everyday life and relationships

CWR, Waverley Abbey House,
Waverley Lane, Farnham,
Surrey GU9 8EP, UK

Telephone: +44 (0)1252 784700
Email: info@cwr.org.uk
Website: www.cwr.org.uk

Registered Charity No 294387
Company Registration No 1990308